Fantastic Electronics

Build Your Own
Negative-Ion Generator
& Other Projects

Fantastic Electronics
Build Your Own
Negative-Ion Generator
& Other Projects

John Iovine

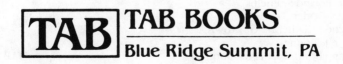

TAB BOOKS
Blue Ridge Summit, PA

FIRST EDITION
FIRST PRINTING

© 1993 by **TAB Books**.
TAB Books is a division of McGraw-Hill, Inc.

Library of Congress Cataloging-in-Publication Data

Iovine, John.
   Fantastic electronics : build your own negative-ion generator &
other projects / by John Iovine.
     p.   cm.
   Includes index.
   ISBN 0-8306-3080-5 (H)   ISBN 0-8306-3079-1
(P)
    1. Electronics—Amateurs manuals.   I. Title.
TK9965.I58   1992
621.3—dc20   92-13042
                                        CIP

TAB Books offers software for sale. For information and a catalog, please contact
TAB Software Department, Blue Ridge Summit, PA 17294-0850.

Acquisitions Editor: Roland S. Phelps
Book Editor: Andrew Yoder
Director of Production: Katherine G. Brown
Book Design: Jaclyn J. Boone
Cover Design: Denny Bond, East Petersburg, Pa.   TAB1

Contents

Introduction   **xi**

1 Recombinant DNA experiment   **1**

Human genome project   *2*
  Biotechnology 101   *2*
  Genes   *3*
  Nucleic acids   *3*
  The genetic code   *7*
  Transfer RNA (tRNA)   *7*
  Ribosomal RNA (rRNA)   *7*
  Clones   *9*
  Genetic manipulation by viruses   *10*
  First step toward genetic engineering   *11*
  Recombinant DNA   *12*
  Restriction endonuclease enzymes   *13*
  Making E. coli competent   *14*
  Plasmid vector   *15*
Gene splicing experiment   *15*
  Overview   *15*
  98.6°F incubator   *17*
  107.6°F water bath   *18*
  Ligation of DNA   *20*
  Transform E. coli with recombinant DNA   *21*

2 Genetic evolution   **27**

Procedures   *27*
Experiment 1   *28*

Experiment 2   *28*
Experiment 3   *30*
Evolution and sex   *30*

3 Negative ion generator   33

Ion effect   *33*
Additional research   *34*
Ion generator   *36*

4 Bio-feedback/lie-detector device   39

Circuit description   *39*
Bio-feedback section   *40*
Electrodes   *41*
Circuit construction   *42*
Circuit operation   *43*
Bio-feedback   *44*
Lie detector   *44*

5 ELF monitor   45

Why wasn't it sooner?   *45*
The real deal   *46*
The evidence   *47*
Not all the news is bad   *48*
Computer monitors   *48*
Tale of the tape   *49*
Shielding   *49*
Precautions around the home   *50*
ELF monitor   *52*
Construction   *54*
Calibration   *55*
Using the ELF monitor   *55*

6 Hydrophone   57

Hydrophone specifications   *57*
Audio amplifier   *58*
Use   *59*

7 Geiger counter project   63

Radioactivity   *63*
Background radiation   *63*
History   *64*
Measurement of radioactivity   *65*
The circuit   *67*

Construction *68*
Radioactive sources *70*
Checking and troubleshooting *70*
Other Geiger tubes *71*
Inverse square law *71*
Detecting solar flares *72*
Sources *73*

8 MHD generator   **75**

MHD basics *75*
Making a plasma *75*
Advantages of MHD generators *76*
MHD model *77*
Operation *78*
Improving the MHD generator *79*
Liquid metal MHD *79*
MHD propulsion *79*
How MHD propulsion works *80*

9 Plasma acoustics   **83**

Basic operation *83*
How it works *84*
Experimenting with plasma acoustics *84*
Improving the design *87*
Other experiments *87*

10 Expansion cloud chamber   **89**

Construction *89*
Radioactive source *90*
Use *90*
Suppliers for radioactive materials *92*

11 Nitinol-shaped memory alloy   **93**

History *93*
Applications *94*
How it works *94*
Properties *95*
Wire diameter *96*
Activating nitinol wire *96*
Direct electric heating *96*
Pulse-width modulation heating *97*
Circuit *97*
Nitinol demonstration *97*

Use   *99*
2nd demonstration model   *100*
Going further   *100*

12 Air-pollution monitor   **105**
Semiconductor sensor   *105*
  Gases detected by the sensor   *105*
Future sensors   *106*
  Sensor characteristics   *107*
Test circuit   *108*
  Simple air-pollution monitor   *109*
Going further   *110*

13 Neural networks   **113**
Biological neurons   *114*
  Human brain   *115*
Sun-tracker neural circuit   *118*
  Other uses   *120*

14 Introduction to stepper motors   **123**
Basic operations   *123*
  Resolution   *124*
  Other types of stepper motors   *125*
The real world   *125*
Test circuit   *129*
  Stepper motor   *130*
  Test circuit demonstration   *130*
  Troubleshooting   *132*

15 Equatorial camera mount for astrophotography   **133**
Construction   *135*
  Camera arm   *137*
  The circuit   *137*
  Flexible shaft   *140*
  Battery   *142*
  Use   *142*
  Light pollution   *144*

16 Laser power supply for holography   **147**
Holography versus photography   *148*
  Redundancy   *149*
  Lasers   *151*
Laser power supply   *152*

How the supply works   *153*
Connecting the power supply to the laser   *153*
Testing and calibrating the laser power supply   *154*
Laser tube housing   *155*
Laser safety   *157*

17   Holography part II   **159**

Isolation table   *159*
Optical components and mounts   *161*
  Securing optical components   *162*
Film   *162*
  Film plate holder   *163*
Safelight   *163*
Shooting your first hologram   *164*
  Choosing an object   *164*
  Making the exposure   *166*
  Developing your hologram   *166*
  Viewing your hologram   *167*
  Troubleshooting   *170*
  Hints and tips   *170*
  Disposing of spent chemicals   *171*
  One more for the road   *171*
Going further   *172*

18   Kirlian photography   **175**

Short history   *175*
  Usefulness   *176*
  Debunking the myths   *176*
  Cold electron emission   *176*
Circuit operation   *176*
Circuit construction   *177*
  Exposure plate   *178*
Exposures   *180*
  Film   *181*

19   Pinhole photography   **183**

History of pinhole optics   *183*
Pinhole camera   *184*
  The pinhole   *185*
  F-stop   *187*
  Making your pinhole   *187*
  Finishing the camera   *188*
Pinhole darkroom   *188*
  Loading the camera   *189*

Exposure   *189*
Simple development   *190*
Going further   *194*
ISO multiply exposure time   *194*

20 Oil and gas from coal   195

Synthetic gasoline and oil   *195*
Making fuel gas from coal   *196*
Buying coal   *196*
Caution   *197*
Making synthetic gas and oil from coal   *198*
Second method for producing synthetic gas   *198*
Going further   *198*

21 Alcohol fuel production   201

Sugar concentration, pH, and temperature   *202*
Reaction vessel   *202*
Fermentation lock   *202*
Fuel grade   *205*
2-cycle engines   *205*
U.S. government regulations   *206*
Going further   *206*

22 Bio-gas generation   207

Bio-gas composition   *207*
Plant fertilizer   *207*
Anaerobic fermentation   *208*
Test experiment   *208*
Going further   *211*

23 Wood as fuel   213

Experimental gas generator   *213*

Index   215

Introduction

*S*ometimes I am asked, "Where do you get your ideas for projects to write about?" My answer is simple. I write what I would like to read. This book contains science experiments that I would like to read about.

Many of the projects in this book touch upon technologies that have far-reaching implications in the near future (such as recombinant DNA, genetic evolution, and holography). Other projects apply old technology to new problems (such as waste disposal, conservation, recycling, and energy generation), which are illustrated in the bio-gas, coal gasification, alcohol fuel production and wood experiments.

The experiments provide you with a beginning inroad into exciting areas of science. It is up to you, if you choose, to blaze your own trail.

Chapter 1

Recombinant DNA experiment

*G*ene manipulation is a relatively new science. Companies are pursuing genetic engineering to develop medicines and vaccines that are safer and more effective than conventional products. As an example, genetically engineered bacteria have produced human life-saving proteins, such as insulin and interferon.

Biotechnology has passed the stage of just using bacteria to produce human proteins. British researchers are using cows, endowed with foreign DNA to produce pharmaceuticals in their milk. These genetically engineered cows are capable of reproducing and transmitting the genetic code to their offspring. New advances in growth hormones will increase milk production in cows, reduce fat in pigs, and bring poultry to market faster.

Plants that produce fruits and vegetables also benefit from genetic engineering. They can be made with more resistance to attack from bacteria and insects. In some cases, they produce their own pesticides. Other benefits include tomatoes that have been engineered to ripen twice as long as normal. As a result of this gene manipulation, the tomatoes will stay fresh on the long trip from the farm to the market. The U.S. government approved this procedure and deemed other genetically altered plants safe for marketing and human consumption on May 27, 1992. We can expect to see these genetically manipulated tomatoes for sale starting in 1993.

HUMAN GENOME PROJECT

It has been estimated that it will cost 3 billion dollars and 15 years to map and identify the 100,000 genes within the humans' 46 chromosomes. This is equivalent to mapping approximately 3 billion base pairs of DNA. It is hoped that gathering this information will help scientists to diagnose and treat inherited disorders. In addition, it might provide inroads to curing diseases, such as cancer and AIDS.

We already benefit from genetic technology. Genetic tests are currently given during a woman's pregnancy to check for genetic disorders. Recently, the U.S. government made plans to sample DNA from every person in military service to make a DNA fingerprint. The DNA fingerprints will be used for identification if, in the case of war or an unfortunate accident, standard identification is impossible. Future tombs of "the unknown soldier" will not be necessary.

Biotechnology 101

Before you get to manipulating genetic information for yourself, first review some basic biology. Protein molecules are made up of subunits, called *amino acids*. Two linked amino acids are a *peptide*. Larger amino acid molecules are *polypeptides*. A protein is a *polypeptide molecule*.

Amino acids are built from atoms of carbon, hydrogen, oxygen, nitrogen, and occasionally sulfur. The 20 different types of amino acids are:

Amino Acid	Abbreviation	Amino Acid	Abbreviation
Glycine	GLY	Arginine	ARG
Alanine	ALA	Asparagine	ASN
Valine	VAL	Glutamine	GLN
Leucine	LEU	Cystine	CYS
Isoleucine	ILE	Methionine	MET
Serine	SER	Phenylalanine	PHE
Threonine	THR	Tyrosine	TYR
Aspartic Acid	ASP	Tryptophan	TRP
Glutamic Acid	GLU	Histidine	HIS
Lysine	LYS	Proline	PRO

Amino acids can be linked in any order. Any change in the order will create a molecule with its own individual properties. For instance, hemoglobin contains 539 amino acids. If you alter just one amino acid out of its proper order it would severely affect the oxygen-carrying capacity (i.e., resulting in sickle cell anemia).

Enzymes are protein molecules that promote a chemical reaction. *Enzyme* is the term used to describe any biological catalyst that is associated with living tissue. Enzymes control all chemical reactions in the cell. Enzymes, like physical catalysts, are unchanged by the reaction they promote and can be reused. Enzymes can take apart or put together molecules.

The particular enzymes that a cell manufactures determine what type of cell it is: whether it's a heart cell, brain cell, or liver cell.

Genes

For many years, it was believed that proteins communicated the genetic information from generation to generation. Although DNA had been looked at as a possible mechanism, it was dismissed as being too simple in structure, being composed of just four nucleic acids, to relay the complex biological messages. Proteins on the other hand, use 20 different amino acids. So, it was felt that the 20 amino acids provided a more diverse and complex chemical language to transfer genetic information. This turned out to be wrong. The simpler nucleic acids in DNA transmit genetic information.

Nucleic acids

The two kinds of nucleic acids are *Deoxyribonucleic Acid (DNA)* and *Ribonucleic Acid (RNA)*. Nucleic acid molecules are made up of simpler units, *nucleotides*. A nucleotide is in turn made up of three components: sugar, phosphate, and a base (see FIG. 1-1). There is one type of phosphate; two types of sugar (ribose and deoxyribose, see FIG. 1-2) and five types of bases.

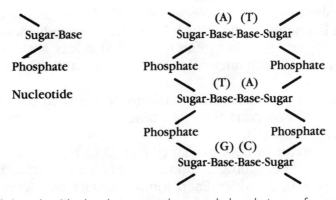

1-1   (A) A nucleotide showing a sugar, base, and phosphate as a free molecule and (B) in a DNA ladder.

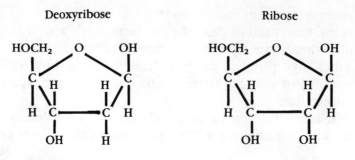

1-2 Sugar molecules, (A) deoxyribose and (B) ribose.

Base	Abbreviation	
Adenine	A	
Thymine	T	found exclusively in DNA
Guanine	G	
Cytosine	C	
Uracil	U	found exclusively in RNA

Nucleic acids, whether it's DNA or RNA, are made up of just four nucleotides. In addition, just one type of sugar molecule is used in a particular acid; ribose is used exclusively in RNA and deoxyribose in DNA.

Double helix   In the early 1950s, Rosalind Frankin took a sharp x-ray diffraction photograph of the DNA molecule. The diffraction pattern suggested a helical molecule with a repeat pattern of 34 A and a width of 20 A.

James Watson and Francis Crick used this information to work out the structure of the DNA molecule in 1953. The structure of the DNA molecule is a double helix, which looks like a twisted ladder or a spiral staircase (see FIG. 1-3). To extend the twisted ladder analogy, the sugar and phosphate of each nucleotide form the legs, and the bases form the crossbars.

There is a complementary relationship between the nucleotides. Adenine (A) always pairs with Thymine (T), and Cytosine (C) always pairs with guanine (G).

The structure of DNA explained how DNA replicated itself during cell division. The hydrogen bonds between the nucleotides break, unzipping the DNA ladder. Each complementary half serves as a template for reconstructing the other half. The results are two identical DNA molecules.

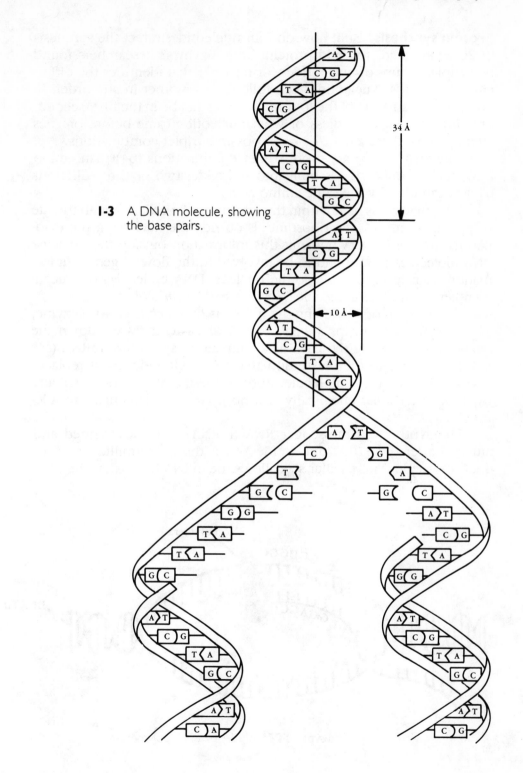

1-3 A DNA molecule, showing the base pairs.

Protein synthesis   Still, how do four nucleotides direct the synthesis of 20 amino acids to build proteins and enzymes? Researchers found that triplet groups of nucleotides form a code that identifies the different amino acids. Nucleotides can follow one another in any order. In other words, any one of the four nucleotides can be in the first, second, or third position, regardless of what nucleotide came before or goes after it. Thus, there are $4 \times 4 \times 4 = 64$ possible triplet combinations.

Obviously, there are more triplet combinations (64) than amino acids (20). Redundancy is built into the code; two or three different triplets can identify the same amino acid.

DNA material is held within the nucleus of the cell, although the site of protein synthesis, the ribosome, is outside the nucleus in the cytoplasm. How does DNA transmit this information outside the nucleus? RNA molecules were found to be involved in the flow of genetic information from inside to outside the nucleus. DNA molecules produce a complementary RNA molecule, *messenger RNA (mRNA)*.

The process of producing the mRNA is *transcription*. An enzyme, RNA polymerase, unzips a small region of DNA. It travels down the strand of DNA, using the DNA as a template to synthesize mRNA (see FIG. 1-4). Notice in the illustration that the nucleotide uracil replaces thymine in the mRNA molecule. Both of these nucleotides, uracil and thymine, are similar chemically and both are complementary to Adenine.

The synthesized messenger RNA (mRNA) is single-stranded and much shorter (50−1000 nucleotides) than the DNA (million nucleotides) molecule. This smaller size allows the mRNA to pass through the

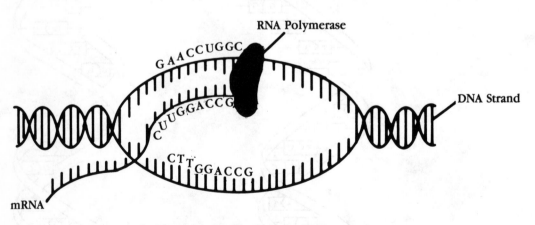

1-4   The synthesis of mRNA by RNA polymerase.

nucleus membrane into the cytoplasm. It is mRNA that brings the DNA information outside the nucleus for protein synthesis.

The genetic code

So far so good, the mRNA brings the information outside the nucleus for protein synthesis. We now need to know how that information is coded and synthesized. The triplet nucleotides that code specific amino acids are *codons*. The codons are abbreviated using the first letter of the base in the particular nucleotide. The codon AUG, for example, represents the bases Adenine-Uracil-Guanine. The task to find which triplet identified which amino acid became known as "cracking the genetic code."

The first break in the code occurred in 1961. Researchers Nirenberg and Matther found that a synthetic mRNA molecule consisting only of uracil (making codons UUU-UUU-UUU-UUU . . .) produced a polypeptide consisting of the amino acid phenylalanine. Soon, all codon combinations were produced, creating a genetic dictionary.

Most proteins begin with the amino acid methionine, its codon is AUG. This codon also represents the start signal for protein synthesis. The three codons UAA, UAG, and UGA do not represent any amino acid, rather they are stop signals that terminate a protein synthesis.

Of all the amino acids, just two (methionine and tryptophanare) specified by a single codon. All other amino acids are specified by two or more codons. For example, the amino acid glycine is identified by any codon that begins with GG, regardless of the nucleotide in the third position. Figure 1-5 illustrates the entire genetic code.

Transfer RNA (tRNA)

Transfer RNA (tRNA) molecules perform the actual translation. The tRNA has three unpaired bases, the *anti-codon*, on one end of the molecule. These bases are complementary to the codon bases. When the anti-codon on the tRNA matches the codon on the mRNA, it binds with the codon on the mRNA strand. On the opposite end of the tRNA molecule is a site that can attach a single amino acid specified by the codon (see FIG. 1-6). For each tRNA, there is a specific amino acid that can bind to its site.

Ribosomal RNA (rRNA)

The ribosome (ribosomal RNA) travels down the mRNA strand, linking the amino acids attached to the tRNA into a protein. As each amino acid is linked, the empty tRNA is released (see FIG. 1-7). The released tRNA is

Second base

		U	C	A	G	
First base	U	UUU UUC } PHE UUA UUG } LEU	UCU UCC UCA UCG } SER	UAU UAC } TYR UAA UAG } STOP	UGU UGL } CYS UGA STOP UGG TRP	U C A G
	C	CUU CUC CUA CUG } LEU	CCU CCC CCA CCG } PRO	CAU CAC } AIS CAA CAG } GLN	CGU CGC CGA CGG } ARG	U C A G
	A	AUU AUC } ILE AVA AVG MET*	ACU ACC ACA ACG } THR	AAU AAC } ASN AAA AAG } LYS	AGU AGC } SER AGA AGG } ARG	U C A G
	G	GUU GUC GUA GUG } VAL	GCU GCC GCA GCG } AUA	GAU GAC } ASP GAA GAG } GLU	GGU GGC GGA GGG } GLY	U C A G

Third base

*Start signal for protein synthesis

1-5 The genetic code.

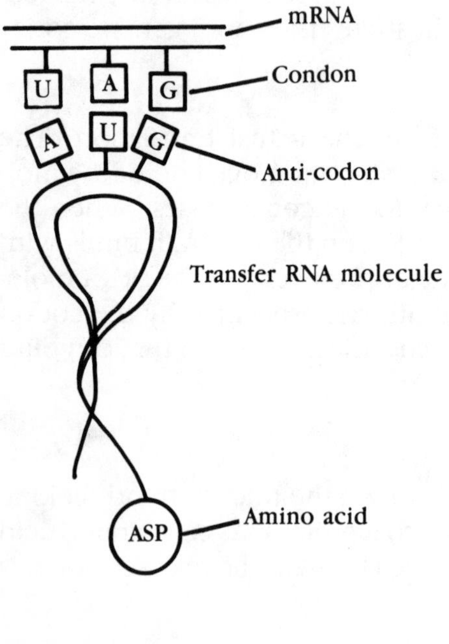

Transfer RNA molecule   **1-6** tRNA and mRNA in protein synthesis.

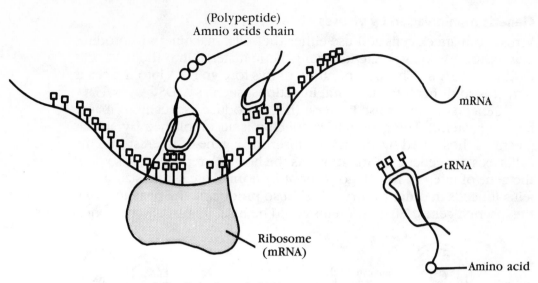

(Polypeptide)
Amnio acids chain

mRNA

tRNA

Ribosome
(mRNA)

Amino acid

I-7 Overview of rRNA protein synthesis.

able to pick up an amino acid and again bind to a site on the mRNA strand.

The ribosome begins protein synthesis by attaching itself to the codon AUG, which (as stated before) is the codon for methionine and also the start message for protein synthesis. It continues linking amino acids together until it reaches one of the stop codons UAA, UAG, or UGA, which terminates synthesis. The completed protein is then released from the ribosome to perform its function.

Clones

Bacteria usually reproduce through asexual reproduction and are clones. The DNA from the parent cell is replicated, with identical genetic information, which is passed on to the daughter cells. Successive generation of cells in turn divide and quickly give rise to a population of genetically identical clones; all cells are derived from a single ancestral cell. The idea of cloning a human from the DNA in one of its cells is possible, and makes for a good science-fiction plot, but it is still a number of years away from being practical.

E. coli is a favorite bacteria used in genetic engineering. It is part of the normal bacterial flora that inhabits the human colon. Under ideal conditions, E. coli can replicate itself once every 22 minutes. In just 11 hours, one cell can go through 30 generations and create more than one billion cells.

Genetic manipulation by viruses

Viruses can attack cells and use either the cells' machinery to produce new viruses or incorporate its own genetic material into the host cells DNA (see FIG. 1-8). The incorporation of this foreign DNA into the cell is why it is so difficult to cure viral infections, such as AIDS.

Genetic engineers use bacteria that reproduce asexually to manufacture proteins. The gene (DNA) splicing is accomplished by similar means of those used by viruses, by inserting a gene of interest into the cell's existing genetic information. As the host cell reproduces, so does the gene of interest. As cell goes about its normal life synthesizing proteins it needs in order to survive, it's also producing the proteins from the inserted genes. These proteins could be insulin, growth hormones,

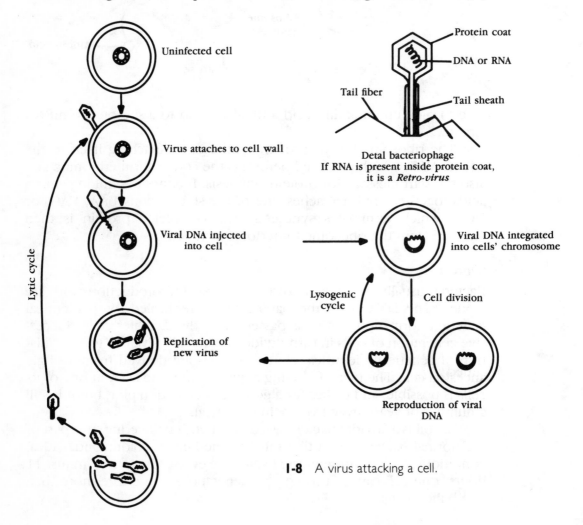

1-8 A virus attacking a cell.

interferon, or any genetic information that can be spliced into the cell DNA successfully.

First step toward genetic engineering

In the 1950s, it was found that a certain strain of Escherichia coli (E. coli) could protect themselves from introduced foreign DNA. These cells had a primitive immune system (see FIG. 1-9). The E. coli possesses an enzyme system that selectively destroys foreign DNA, but leaves its own DNA intact.

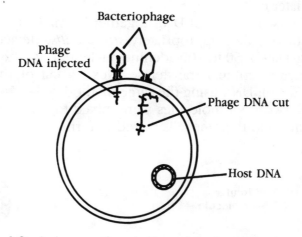

1-9 A close-up of a primitive cellular immune system.

This protective enzyme was extracted and analyzed. This enzyme was the first "restriction endonuclease" discovered. The enzyme worked by cutting the foreign DNA into pieces. In essence, restriction endonuclease enzymes are molecular scalpels that can cut DNA.

In 1970, researchers Smith and Wilcox isolated another restriction endonuclease enzyme from Haemophilus influenza. The enzyme was named *HindII*. The difference with this new enzyme is that it cut DNA at predictable points, within a recognition sequence of nucleotides. This is in contrast to the other enzymes, which cut the DNA pretty much at random points.

Daniel Nathans used the HindII enzyme to cut the DNA of a small virus that infects monkeys, called *simian virus 40 (SV40)*. In doing so, he created a restriction map of the virus that showed where the enzyme cut the DNA.

Recombinant DNA

In 1972, Paul Berg worked out a method of joining DNA molecules. Using the restriction enzyme EcoRI, he cut the circular DNA of the SV40 virus and a small circular DNA molecule from E. coli. The restriction enzyme cut each molecule at a single point, opening the circular DNA to form strands (see FIG. 1-10).

The DNA molecule from E. coli is particularly important. The DNA molecule used, exists apart from the bacteria's main chromosomes. The small DNA molecule, a *plasmid*, has the ability to replicate and produce proteins on its own. The plasmid vector will be explained in greater detail later on.

To join the two strands of DNA together he made the ends of the DNA strand sticky, called appropriately *sticky ends*. He accomplished this by adding a tail of 50 to 100 adenine nucleotides to the SV40 virus using the enzyme terminal transferase. Next, a tail of thymine was added to the E. Coli DNA using the same method.

When the two DNA molecules were mixed together, the complementary adenine and thymine tails paired to form one circular, recom-

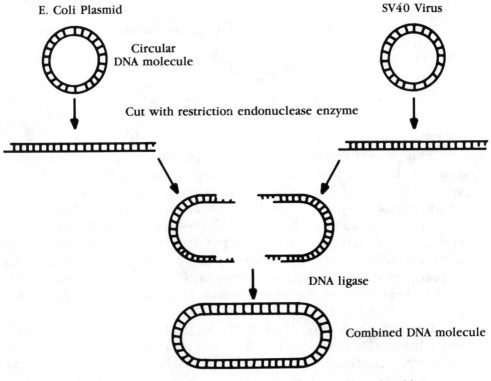

1-10 The procedure for combining SV40 virus with a plasmid.

binant DNA molecule. Two other enzymes were used to finish the job. DNA polymerase filled any single-stranded gaps and DNA ligase sealed the junction points (see FIG. 1-11). Later, it was found out that EcoRI produced its own sticky ends, eliminating the need to add tails to the DNA strands.

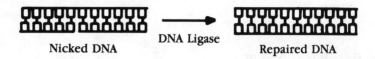

Nicked DNA   **DNA Ligase**   Repaired DNA

1-11 How ligase repairs breaks in DNA.

Paul Berg's experiment illustrated that a restriction enzyme could be used to cut DNA in a predictable and controlled manner and that the DNA fragments from different organisms could be joined together. In 1973, Stanley Cohen and Annie Chang took Berg's experiment further. They inserted the recombinant plasmid back into the E. coli bacteria where it was maintained and replicated along with the cell.

Restriction endonuclease enzymes

There are three major classes of restriction endonuclease. Types I and III cut DNA at sites a distance away from their recognition sequences. ATP must be provided so that these enzymes have enough energy to work.

The enzyme used most often is the Type II. These enzymes cut DNA in a predictable manner on or adjacent to the recognition site. The energy required is supplied by a simple magnesium ion ($Mg++$). Currently, there are over 1200 type II restriction endonuclease enzymes.

The names of these enzymes are coded as follows:

1. The first letter is usually the initial letter of the organism from where the enzyme is collected.

2. The second and third letters are usually the organism's species name.

3. The fourth letter, if any, indicates the strain.

4. The Roman numeral usually indicates the order of discovery.

EcoRI breaks down as follows:

  E   Genus escherichia
  co Species coli

    R   Strain RY13
    I   First endonuclease isolated

HindIII breaks down to:

    H   Genus Haemophilus
    in   Species influenza
    d   Strain RD
    III Third endonuclease isolated

Making E. coli competent

Competent is a term used to describe cells brought into the proper physiological state so that they can absorb molecules of foreign DNA from the environment. In 1970, Mandel and Higg found that E. coli becomes competent when the cells are suspended in a cold calcium chloride solution and subjected to a brief heat shock (see FIG. 1-12) at 42 °C (106 °F).

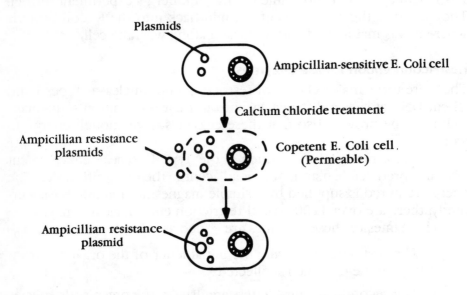

Plasmids

Ampicillian-sensitive E. Coli cell

Calcium chloride treatment

Ampicillian resistance plasmids

Copetent E. Coli cell. (Permeable)

Ampicillian resistance plasmid

Transformed Ampicillian resistance E. Coli cell

I-12 The procedure for making E. coli competent for transformation.

The precise mechanism of DNA uptake by competent E. coli cells is at the moment unknown. In any case, this method is used in the following experiment.

Plasmid vector

In standard medical terminology, a vector is an organism that carries a disease from one host organism to another. In genetic engineering, a vector is a DNA molecule that carries an inserted gene into a host cell.

The plasmid vector used in this experiment is from E. coli. Plasmid vectors range in size from 1000 to 200,000 base pairs (bp). It is a circular or looped DNA molecule. The advantage to using plasmid DNA is that it exists separately from E. coli's main chromosome. In addition, it has the ability to replicate itself within the cell and be propagated through successive bacterial generations.

The plasmid structure within the host cell contains the information to synthesize proteins. In this experiment, it will contain the information to synthesize the protein from the gene (DNA) instructions that you inserted into it.

One of the plasmid vectors that you will be making is called the *pAMP*. This plasmid has the instructions (DNA) to synthesize antibiotic ampicillin inserted into its DNA. An overview of the making of a pAMP plasmid vector is illustrated in FIG. 1-13. Although the chemicals are available for splicing our own plasmids and inserting a gene, you can also purchase a kit with plasmid vectors and antibiotic genes ready to be joined together and inserted into a bacterial cell.

GENE SPLICING EXPERIMENT

Although the materials in the kit are safe, it is important for you to follow the simple procedures to keep the experiment controlled and non-threatening.

We are working with Escherichia coli (E. coli) bacteria, a favorite of gene splicers everywhere. It is not a pathogenic bacteria. In fact, it is part of the normal bacteria flora that exists in your colon. It is rarely associated with any disease.

Overview

First, you will construct three types of vector plasmids. One plasmid will contain an antibiotic resistance gene for ampicillin, *pAMP*. The second will contain a gene for the resistance of the antibiotic kanamycin, *pKAN*. The third will contain the genes of both, *pAMP/pKAN*.

The plasmid fractions are mixed with DNA ligase to form stable recombinant DNA. Next, use the calcium chloride procedure to inject and transform the E. coli bacteria with the recombinant DNA. To test

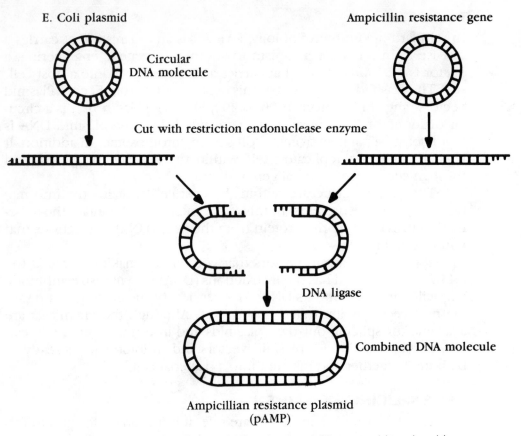

1-13 The procedure for combining the Ampicillin gene with a plasmid.

our bacteria for uptake of the recombinant DNA, culture the bacteria on specific agar plates. One plate has ampicillin, another has kanamycin, the third has both ampicillin and kanamycin mixed in the agar, the fourth plate is plain nutrient agar.

Only the bacteria that has been transformed can grow on the antibiotic-treated agar. Our control E. coli group, which remains untransformed, will not grow on the antibiotic-treated plates, but the transformed bacteria will.

As stated, you can purchase all the materials necessary separately to do this and other DNA experiments or you can purchase a kit. I strongly advise to purchase the kit (see the index of suppliers).

The kit includes:

Vial plasmid pAMP   12 needle-point pipets
Vial plasmid pKAN   18 1-ml sterile transfer pipets

3 vials ligase/ligation   4 15-ml sterile culture tubes
Culture E. coli   5 sterile inoculating loops
1 vial calcium chloride   Glass cell spreader
3 LB agar plates   Manual
2 LB AMP agar plates
2 LB KAN agar plates
2 LB AMP/KAN agar plates

The kit supplies all the tubes, pipets, plates, cultures, and regents needed for this experiment. When you receive the kit in the mail, refrigerate the culture plates (upside down) and the vials of plasmid pAMP, pKAN, and calcium chloride. Freeze the vial of ligase/ligate buffer/ATP. The other materials can be stored at room temperature.

In addition to the materials provided in the kit, you also need: 70 to 95% ethanol alcohol, a small quantity of distilled water, a marker for labeling culture plates and tubes, a beaker or dish, a 98.6°F incubator, 106°F water bath, crushed ice, a small quantity of household bleach, an alcohol lamp or a bunsen burner.

98.6°F incubator

Because E. coli inhabits the human gut, it is not surprising that the optimum temperature for its growth is human body temperature, 98.6°F. You can use any enclosed space for an incubator. If you don't have such an area, a 20-gallon glass aquarium will do nicely. Place the aquarium on its side with the open end facing you. Tape a piece of plastic to the top of the aquarium so that the plastic drapes down and covers the open end of the aquarium (see FIG. 1-14). Secure the plastic to just the top of the aquarium; in order to work inside, you will need to lift the plastic up and out of the way.

To heat the incubator to 98.6°F, I used a standard incandescent lamp, placed in the aquarium, with the lamp enclosed in a can or small pail to block the light (*Note:* light doesn't affect the growth of E. coli). I needed a 75-watt bulb to warm the incubator to 92°F. This temperature is lower than the optimum temperature, but it works fine. Start out using a 40-watt bulb and measure the temperature after 12 to 24 hours. Increase the wattage if it is necessary. If the incubator becomes hotter than 98.6°F, reduce the wattage of the bulb. If it is impossible to adjust the temperature by just changing the wattage of the bulb, insert a light dimmer control to the bulb. Use the light dimmer to adjust the power to the lamp and consequentially the temperature. It is better to keep the temperature a little lower than 98.6°F, than above that mark.

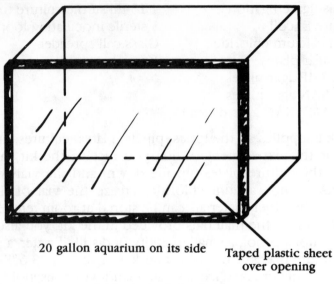

20 gallon aquarium on its side   Taped plastic sheet
over opening

1-14 A simple incubator.

It's a good idea to set up your incubator and adjust the temperature before the kit arrives. This way, you can start on it right away.

107.6°F water bath

You only need the water bath once for 90 seconds to heat shock the
bacteria. You can use an aquarium heater to bring the water to this temperature. In a pinch, just run tap water and adjust the temperature with
a thermometer to 107°F. Adjust it and keep the water running into a
small container. Use water in the container to heat shock the bacteria.

Simple procedures Wash your hands with an anti-bacterial soap
before and after working with the materials. Keep the work space and
incubator spotless. Wipe the area with a 10% bleach solution or a disinfectant (such as Lysol™).

Wear protective goggles and gloves. Disinfect all materials after use
(such as tubes, pipets, and transfer loops), by placing them in 10%
bleach solution.

Starter plate Our first step is to incubate and grow E. coli strain bacteria on an agar culture plate. We need the colonies grown on this plate
for the rest of the experiment.

1. Take one plain LB agar plate and mark the bottom of the plate
   "E. coli." Indicate the date in which you streaked the plate.

2. Sterilize the wire inoculating loop in the flame of the alcohol lamp or bunsen burner. Allow the wire to get red hot, then remove it from flame. Hold the loop for a few seconds for it to cool, and do not touch the inoculating loop or place it down because this would contaminate it.

3. Hold the vial of E. coli culture in the opposite hand and remove the cap. With the cap removed, pass the mouth of vial through flame to sterilize it. Do not stop and hold the vial in the flame, this might cause the vial to shatter.

4. Push the inoculating loop into the side of agar to cool the loop. Then, drag the loop a few times across the area of E. coli culture. Remove the loop, pass the mouth of the vial through the flame again, and recap it.

5. Lift top of agar plate, marked "E. coli," just enough to perform streaking (see FIG. 1-15).

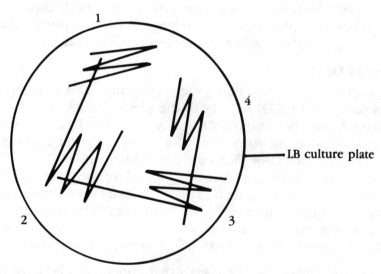

1-15   How to make streaks on a starter plate.

a. Drag the loop back and forth across the agar surface. Do not stab the loop into the agar. Make a few streaks across the top (FIG. 1-15). Replace the lid between streaks.

b. Turn the agar plate 90°. Reflame the loop, cool the loop by stabbing it into the agar plate, away from the first streak. Pass the loop once through the first streak and continue in zig-zag pattern.

    c. Turn the agar plate 90°. Reflame the loop and proceed as before, except draw the loop once through the secondary streak.

    d. Turn the agar plate 90°. Reflame loop and proceed as before, except draw the loop once through the third streak, and make a final zig-zag pattern.

    e. Replace the lid on the culture plate.

6. Reflame the loop before putting it down. This prevents contaminating the work space. Make reflaming the loop a habit.

7. Place the plate upside down in the incubator. This prevents condensation, which might collect on the lid from falling into the agar and smearing the E. coli colonies. Incubate the plate from 12 to 24 hours.

8. After the initial incubation, remove it from the incubator and allow the colonies to grow 1 to 2 days at room temperature (approximately 72 °F), keeping the plates upside down. Do not touch the colonies with your fingers. Do not over incubate the culture or the E. coli will overgrow on the plate.

Ligation of DNA

In this procedure, we are linking the fragmented DNA molecules. The regents pAMP and pKAN have both the plasmid DNA strands from E. coli bacteria, plus the antibiotic DNA fragment. The ligase links the two DNA molecules via the formation of a phosphodiester bond. See the simple structure of a DNA molecule under nucleotides.

    It is interesting to note that this procedure forms many different types of hybrid molecules, such as plasmids that are composed of more than two fragments. However, only those that form properly will be maintained and expressed in the cell. The ATP in the ligation solution provides the energy for the reaction that joins the nucleotides together.

1. You will need the three vials that contain the 20 μl of ligation buffer ATP/ligase. Label one tube ''+pAMP/KAN,'' label another ''+pAMP,'' and label the last tube ''+pKAN.''

2. To measure quantities, use a sterile needle-nose pipet (see FIG. 1-16). Use a fresh needle-nose for each regent.

    a. To the +pAMP/KAN tube, add 10 μl of pAMP and 10 μl of pKAN.

    b. To the +pAMP tube, add 10 μl of pAMP and 10 μl of distilled water.

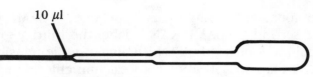

1-16 A detail of the needle-nose pipet.

    c. To the +pKAN tube, add 10 μl of pKAN and 10 μl of distilled water.

3. Close tube tops and gently tap tube bottoms on table to mix regents.

4. Incubate tubes at room temperature for 2 to 24 hours (see FIG. 1-17).

Transform E. coli with recombinant DNA

In this procedure, you are making the E. Coli cells competent, which allows the cells to uptake the recombinant DNA that you made in the preceding procedure.

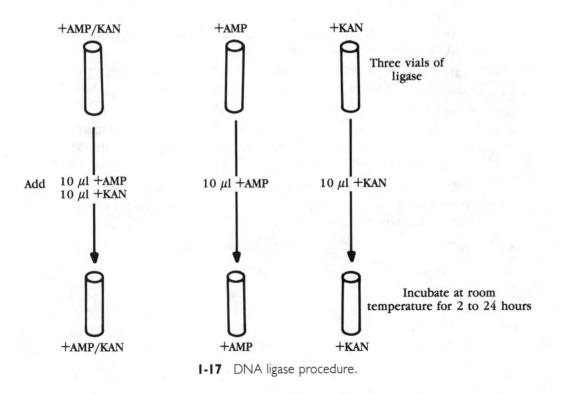

1-17 DNA ligase procedure.

1. Get four sterile 15-ml tubes. Label one "+pAMP/KAN," label the second "−pAMP/KAN," label the third "+pAMP," and label the fourth "+pKAN." Using a sterile transfer pipet (see FIG. 1-18), add 250 µl of cold calcium chloride to each tube. Place four tubes into a beaker or dish with crushed ice.

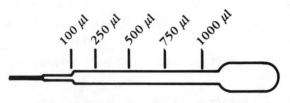

1-18 A detail of the transfer pipet.

2. Using a sterile plastic inoculating loop, transfer one or two colonies of E. coli from the starter plate to the +pAMP/KAN tube. Be careful not to transfer any agar from the plate along with the cell colonies.

   a. Immerse the loop into the calcium chloride solution. Tap against the side of the tube to dislodge the cell mass.

   b. Suspend cells in the solution by repeatedly pipeting in and out with a sterile transfer pipet. Return the +pAMP/KAN tube to ice and discard the pipet.

3. Transfer the cell colony to the −pAMP/KAN tube using the same procedure as described in step 2. Return the −pAMP/KAN tube to the ice and discard the pipet.

4. Transfer the cell colony to the +pAMP tube using the same procedure as described in step 2. Return the +pAMP tube to the ice and discard the pipet.

5. Transfer the cell colony to the +pKAN tube using the same procedure as described in step 2. Return the +pKAN tube to the ice and discard the pipet.

6. Using a fresh needle-nose pipet for each transfer:

   a. Transfer 10 µl of ligated +pAMP/KAN to the +pAMP/KAN culture tube.

   b. Transfer 10 µl of ligated +pAMP to the +pAMP culture tube.

   c. Transfer 10 µl of ligated +pKAN to the +pKAN culture tube.

   d. Do not transfer any material into the −pAMP/KAN culture tube.

7. Place all tubes back in ice and let them incubate on ice for 15 minutes.

8. Following the 15-minute ice incubation, it's time to heat shock the E. coli cells to make them competent. Remove all the tubes from the ice and immediately immerse them in the 107°F water bath for 90 seconds. Then, return all the tubes directly into the ice again. Let these tubes stay on ice for 3 to 4 minutes. If the tubes are immersed in the ice for a longer time period, it will not affect the outcome of the experiment.

9. Using a sterile transfer pipet, add 250 μl of Luria broth (LB) to each tube. Gently tap the tube with your finger to mix the broth and place the tubes in the incubator at 98.6°F for 3 to 6 hours (see FIG. 1-19).

10. Wash your hands.

Plating the results In this procedure, you will check to see if you have successfully incorporated the recombinant DNA into the E. coli bacteria. The culture plates supplied with the kit are marked showing the agar medium.

1. Using the plates supplied in the kit, label them as follows:
    a. Label one LB plate "+"
        Label one LB plate "−"
        Label one LB/AMP/KAN plate "+pAMP/KAN"
        Label one LB/AMP/KAN plate "−pAMP/KAN"
        Label one LB/AMP plate "+pAMP"
        Label one LB/AMP plate "+pKAN"
        Label one LB/KAN plate "+pKAN"
        Label one LB/KAN plate "+pAMP"

2. Using a sterile transfer pipet, add 100 μl of the cell suspension from the −pAMP/KAN culture tube on the −LB/AMP/KAN plate and another 100 μl on the −LB plate. Spread the cells over the surface of the agar using the following procedure:
    a. Dip the glass spreader in the ethanol alcohol and ignite the alcohol using the bunsen burner or alcohol lamp. After the alcohol burns off of the spreader, it is sterile for use. Use the spreader to evenly distribute the cells over the agar.

3. Using another sterile transfer pipet, add 100 μl of the cell suspension from the +pAMP/KAN culture tube to the +LB/AMP/

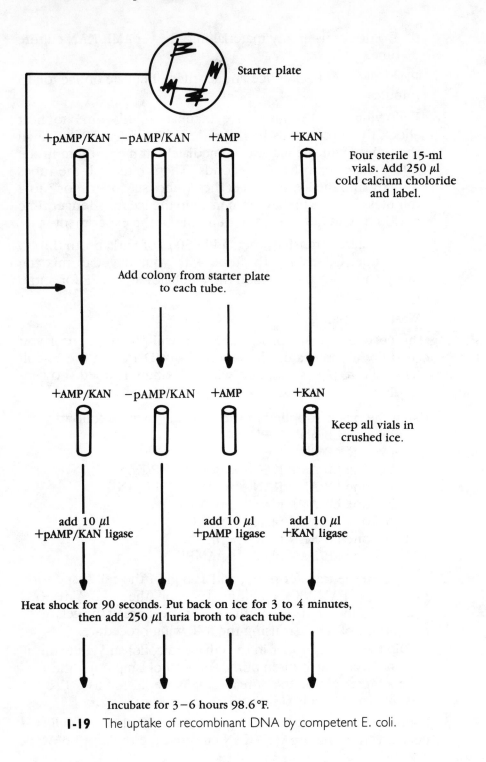

1-19 The uptake of recombinant DNA by competent E. coli.

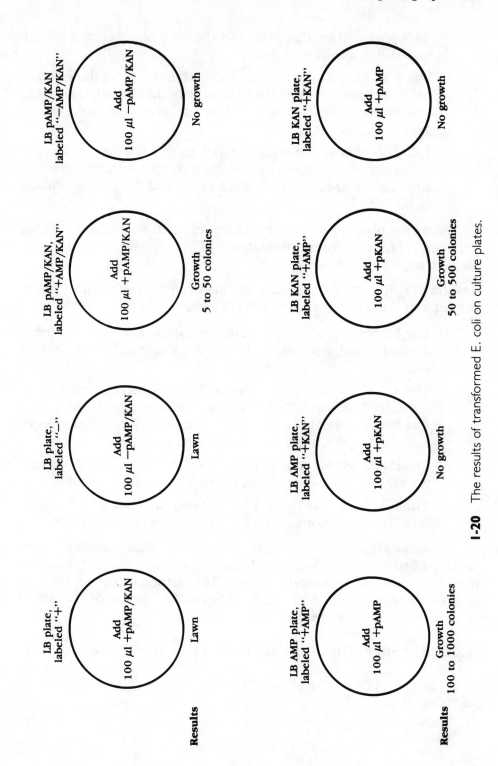

1-20 The results of transformed E. coli on culture plates.

KAN plate and another 100 μl on the +LB plate. Spread the cell suspension as outlined in 2a.

4. Using another sterile transfer pipet add 100 μl of the cell suspension from the +pAMP culture tube to the +pAMP plate, and another 100 μl to the +pKAN plate. Spread the cell suspension as outlined in 2a.

5. Using another sterile transfer pipet, add 100 μl of cell suspension from the +pKAN culture tube to the +pAMP plate and another 100 μl to the +pKAN plate. Spread the cell suspension as outlined in 2a.

Allow the plates to set up for 10 minutes, then wrap them together with tape. Place the plates upside down in 98.6°F incubator. Incubate the plates for 12 to 24 hours.

Results Figure 1-20 illustrates the results of the experiment. If the E. coli growth is too dense to count, record lawn.

1. The LB plates labeled "+" and "−" show that both the transformed E. coli and natural E. coli are viable and grow equally well.

2. The LB plates that contain ampicillin and kanamycin, labeled "+AMP/KAN" and "−AMP/KAN," show that only the E. coli that have been transformed with both antibiotic resistant genes can grow. The natural E. coli fails to grow in this medium.

3. The LB plates that contain the ampicillin, illustrate that the gene for pKAN does not contain a resistant gene for ampicillin.

4. The LB plates that contain kanamycin, illustrate that the gene for pAMP does not contain a resistant gene for kanamycin.

By measuring the growth of the colonies, you can determine that ligation of two genes pAMP and pKAN is more rigorous (5 to 50 colonies) than either single ligation. Further, the ligation of the pKAN gene is more rigorous (50 to 500 colonies) than the ligation of the pAMP gene (100 to 1000 colonies).

E-Z Gene Splicer DNA Recombination and Transformation Kit

CAROLINA BIOLOGICAL SUPPLY COMPANY
2700 York Road
Burlington, NC 27215
(919) 584-0381

Chapter **2**

Genetic evolution

*I*n this experiment, you will trace the evolution of simple yeast cells through genetic mutations. Yeast are unicellular fungi that reproduce asexually through budding. The mutations are manipulated "natural selection" that are caused by placing the yeast in hostile environment, where it must mutate in order to survive.

As with the recombinant DNA experiment, a kit is available, and I advise to purchase the kit rather than buy the materials separately (see the index of suppliers).

The kit includes the following materials:

- 5 labeled culture plates
- A vial of yeast culture
- 4 sterile spreaders
- 4 sterile pipets
- 40 sterile toothpicks

When you receive the kit, refrigerate it until you use it. In addition to the materials in the kit, you will need a marker, paper, a 10% solution of bleach, a disinfectant (such as Lysol™), and antibacterial soap.

PROCEDURES

To keep the experiment accurate and safe, follow these simple procedures:

1. Wash your hands before and after you work with the kit, and use an antibacterial soap.

2. Keep your work area spotless and clean the area with a disinfectant before you begin the experiment.

3. Discard all used materials in a solution of 10% bleach.

The yeast strain that you will be using is Saccharomyces cerevisiae. This yeast strain has a mutation in its ade1 gene. This mutation prevents the synthesis of an enzyme that the yeast requires to make adenine, which (if you remember from the recombinant DNA experiment) is one of the base molecules for DNA. Without this ability to manufacture its own adenine, the yeast cannot reproduce unless adenine is provided.

EXPERIMENT I

Figure 2-1 illustrates the entire experiment. The adenine negative plates do not contain any adenine in the nutrient agar. The copper plates contain copper salts that are poisonous to yeast.

In the first part of the experiment, we inoculate one adenine negative plate and one copper plate with yeast. Only those yeast that mutate can replicate and form colonies on these two "hostile environment" plates. These mutations have been "naturally selected" by their environment.

Shake the vial that contains the yeast cells. Using a sterile pipet, put three drops of yeast culture on the Adenine Negative A plate, and three drops on the Copper A plate. Spread the drops carefully over the surface of the agar using the spreader.

Incubate the plates at room temperature (approximately 72 °F) for 2 to 5 days. Because you are not incubating the culture plates (as we had done in the DNA experiment) you could leave them right side up, but as a matter of habit, you should place them upside down. When colonies appear on the plates, proceed to the second part of the experiment. If you wish to hold off and stop the experiment for a short time, refrigerate the two plates upside down.

EXPERIMENT 2

In this section, we will show that the mutation is transmitted to the offspring, regardless of the fact that the mutation is no longer advantageous or required.

The master culture plate has all the nutrients that yeast requires. No poisons (in the form of copper salts) are added to the agar. Divide the bottom of the master culture plate in two equal halves using your marker. Label one side "adenine" and the other "copper."

Using a sterile toothpick, lift a colony off of the Adenine Negative

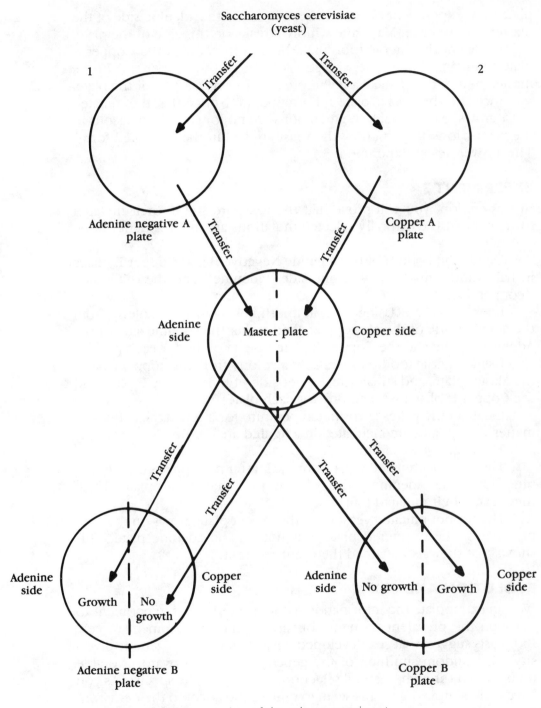

2-1 An overview of the culture experiment.

plate from experiment one, and streak it across the adenine side of the master culture plate. Make a few more streaks on this side of the plate.

Using another sterile toothpick, lift a colony off of the Copper A plate from experiment one, and streak it across the copper side of the master culture plate. Make a few more streaks on this side of the plate.

Incubate the Master plate for a few days. Notice that the mutated yeast grows, even though the mutations are no longer advantageous to the yeast. How do you know the yeast are still in their mutated form? The answer lies in Experiment 3.

EXPERIMENT 3

In this section, you will prove that the yeast are still in their mutated form and that the naturally selected mutations are independent of one another.

Divide the bottom of the Adenine Negative B and Copper B plates in half using a marker. Label one side ''adenine'' and the other side ''copper.''

Look at FIG. 2-1. Using a sterile toothpick, transfer a colony from the adenine side of the Master plate and streak the adenine side of the Adenine B plate and the Copper B plate (use a colony for each plate).

Using a sterile toothpick, transfer a colony from the copper side of the Master plate, and streak the copper side of the Adenine B plate and the Copper B plate (use a colony for each plate).

Incubate the plates at room temperature for a few days. It doesn't matter if the plates are incubated in a lighted area or not.

The results are as follows:

The adenine-mutated yeast from the Master plate grows on the adenine side of the Adenine B plate, but not on the copper plate. Thus, they retain their mutated trait.

The copper-mutated yeast from the Master plate grows on the copper side of the Copper B plate, but not on the adenine plate. This shows that they also retained their mutated trait.

EVOLUTION AND SEX

We can extrapolate the information gathered in this last experiment to question the prevalent thought concerning the development of sex. Biologists suggest that sex developed because it creates a genetic diversity. The random shuffling of the genes can bring forward favorable traits, which through ''natural selection,'' promotes the species. As you have seen, simple organisms seem to mutate and adapt to their environment quite well, without mixing genes though sex.

Evolutionary biologist Richard Michod of the University of Arizona has developed a different possible reason for sex. He believes that sex is used for the species to repair their damaged DNA. The DNA gets damaged naturally through the years of living in the environment: through the food, chemicals, UV from the sun, etc.

It would be highly unlikely for two members of the same species to have their DNA molecules damaged at the same points. So sex got started as a recombination of the two parents' DNA to repair any possible damage being passed to the offsprings' DNA.

Does it wash? Yes. In one experiment, two specific mutated E. coli colonies were grown. One colony's genes were damaged, so it could not synthesize a particular amino acid. For this example, call it Amino Acid A. The other colony had a different gene damaged so that it couldn't synthesize a different amino acid. For this example, call it Amino Acid B.

When both colonies were placed on a culture plate whose nutrient media lacked both amino acids A and B, some colonies formed that could exist on the culture plate.

Apparently the E. coli culture was able to recombine its genes with one another and repair the damaged genes. The process is called *conjugation*, and is analogous to sexual mating in higher organisms.

Yeast Evolution Kit
Cost: $20.00

HERMAN CHIKARMANE
Marine Biological Laboratory
Woods Hole, MA 02543

Chapter 3

Negative
ion generator

*A*ir is the most important ingredient to our survival. Think about it, a person can survive a few days without water, and a little longer without food; but deprived of air to breathe, our survival time can be measured in minutes.

The quality of air, or lack of it, surrounding many cities has become such an important consideration that many local news stations provide an air-quality report along with the weather forecast. Air pollution has become so commonplace that words have been created to describe it. The word *smog*, for example, is a contraction of the words "smoke" and "fog."

Today, there are new questions involving global air quality: the increasing CO_2 level (0.03%), the "greenhouse effect," the ozone-layer depletion, increased UV, acid rain, etc.

Ion effect

Long before there was any talk or concern about air pollution and such, people had a reaction to the quality of air, in regard to its ionization. This idea was popularized by Fred Soyka who wrote a book titled *The Ion Effect* in the 1970s. Mr. Soyka studied natural occurrences of negative and positive ionized air. His findings and inquiries demonstrated that negative ionization had substantial health benefits.

To summarize a few points in this book, negative ions help elevate mood, enhance physical performance and training, and sterilize harmful airborne bacteria. An abundance of positive ions, on the other hand, can be held responsible for a number of low-grade medical problems (such as fatigue, headaches, and anxiety).

Air is composed principally of nitrogen (78%) and oxygen (21%). In addition, air is typically full of positive and negative ions (approximately a 5:4 ratio). When the balance of ions falls heavily into either region, the effects of the air ionization become apparent in biological systems.

Additional research

The first question that entered my mind when I began this project was whether or not those early reports are still considered to be accurate. I answered this question for myself by surveying approximately 100 scientific reports on the effects of negative ions gathered worldwide, from 1973 through the present. I can report that out of my survey approximately 80% of the citings support beneficial effects of negative ions. The remaining reports (greater than 19%) described no effect, and a few (less than 1%) detailed some detrimental effect. Because the preponderance of the evidence still supports positive effects of negative ions, I felt this to be a worthwhile project. Before you begin the actual project, take a look at some of these later reports.

Positive effects Learning enhancement has been noted by researchers in normal and learning disabled children. The task used to test the children was a dichotic listening test.[1]

Negative ions can be used to decrease amounts of radon in building atmosphere.[2]

In one animal study, 1279 calves were broken into two groups, one of 649 head and the remaining 630 head. Negative air ionization was used to test for a prophylactic effectiveness against respiratory diseases. The results were remarkable: In the treated group (649 head), 45 calves became sick and 3 died. In the control group (630 head), 621 became sick and 33 died.[3]

---

[1] *Negative air ion effects on learning disabled and normal achieving children.* Morton, L.L.; Kershner, J.R. University of Windsor, Faculty of Education, Ontario, Canada. 5/90

[2] *Effect of negative ion generators in a sick building.* Finnegan, M.J.; Pickering, C.A.; Gill, F.S.; Aston, I.; and Froese, D. Department of Thoracic Medicine, Wythenshawe Hospital, Manchester, England. 5/87

[3] *Aeroionization in prophylaxis & treatment of respiratory in calves.* Sologub, T.I.; Borzenko, N.F.; Zemlyanskiy, V.P.; and Plakhotnyy, K.F. Russia 1984.

Reduction (40 to 50%) of microbial air pollution in dental clinics has been noted by researchers.[4]

Test using college students showed improved performance on a visual vigilance task.[5]

This list is by no means exhaustive; it's just a sampling of the scientific literature available. However, if this is the case, it would be to our benefit to improve the quality of air that we breathe with a negative ion generator.

Asthma The reports on the effects of negative ions on asthma vary. Some describe beneficial effects, some state no effect, and one claims a negative effect. All the experiments and consequential reports have been performed by reputable scientists. Clearly, additional research must be performed before a determination can be arrived at definitively.

Sports Recently, an article in a popular body-building magazine put forward a theory that negative ions can be used to improve physical performance.[6] It stated further, that Soviet athletes might already be using negative ions, which could explain their superior recuperative powers in athletic meets worldwide (this idea was also reported in Fred Soyka's book).

At least one report that I found does indeed support this hypothesis. In 1983, it was reported that chickens raised in a negative ionized atmosphere showed improved anabolic processes. The chickens raised in negative ionized air had an overall greater weight than the control group. This in spite of the fact that the quality and quantity of the feed were the same for both groups. The meat of the treated group had a higher protein and essential amino acid content. In addition, higher concentrations of vitamins E and A were found in the liver.[7]

No health benefits claimed All commercial negative air ionizers sold in the United States are sold as air purifiers only. Despite the numerous scientific reports to the contrary, no manufacturer of negative ion generators can make any health benefit claims without running

---

[4] *Effect of ionization on microbial air pollution in the dental clinic.* Gabby, J.; Bergerson, O.; Levi, N.; Brenner, S.; and Eli, I. Research Institute for Environment Health, Sackler School of Medicine, Tel Aviv, Israel. 6/90

[5] *Effects of ionized air on the performance of a vigilance task.* Brown, G.C. and Kirk, R.E.; Systems Research Laboratories, Inc., Brooks AFB, TX 6/87.

[6] "Negative Ions." Wright, J.E.; *Muscle & Fitness Magazine*, 1/91

[7] *Effect of Artificial Air Ionization on Broilers.* Stoianov, P.; Petkov, G.; and Baikov, B.D. Vet Med Nauki, 1983, Bulgaria.

afoul with the FDA (neither will I). That is why the documentation supporting this article is listed in the bibliography, for you to verify the research on your own if you wish and to make your own decision.

Susceptibility   Some individuals are more susceptible to the effects of air ionization than others. Regardless of whether you feel any of the reported effects, if the scientific literature is to be believed, an ionizer will in the least help purify the air.

ION GENERATOR

The negative ion generator is fairly straightforward. The main circuit is a high-voltage ac device. The high-voltage lead of the device is connected to a 10-kV high-voltage diode, which permits a negative voltage to pass to a small capacitor bank. This negative high voltage is then connected to a conductive object that has or comes to a sharp point. The sharp point enhances the negative discharge into the surrounding atmosphere. In addition, a small electric fan is incorporated to provide an airflow past the discharge point and into the surrounding air.

You must always be careful when working with high-voltage circuits, such as this. The capacitors might hold a charge for quite a while. When working on the circuit or when troubleshooting, disconnect the power supply and short the capacitors using a wire. Remember to handle the wire by the insulation only or you might get an electrical shock.

The circuit (see FIG. 3-1) uses a standard 555 timer to generate square-wave pulses. The pulses are applied to the base of the TIP 120 npn Darlington transistor. The Darlington provides current to the base of the 3055 power transistor to power the high-voltage auto trans-

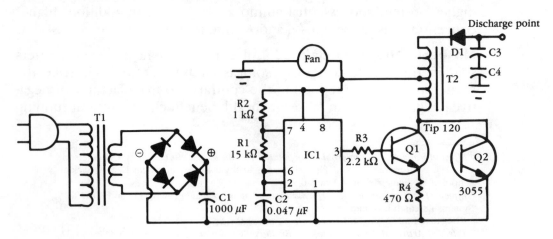

3-1   A schematic of negative ion generator.

former. The high-voltage lead of the transformer is connected to a 10-kV high-voltage diode. Notice the polarity of the diode. It is biased to allow a negative voltage to pass to the high-voltage capacitors and to the discharge needle. For the sharp-pointed object, you can use a sewing needle. An alternative to using a needle for a discharge point is a small piece of 22-gauge stranded wire. Strip off about $1/2$ inch from one end and separate the fine copper wires so that they are evenly dispersed (see FIG. 3-2). Each wire end should now behave as a discharge point. The other end of the wire connects to the negative high-voltage lead.

3-2 A top-view of the ion generator.

You can use any enclosure large enough to hold all of the components. I'd recommend using a plastic enclosure, if one is available. The fan is situated in the enclosure to pull air in past the discharge point(s) and out through the opening hole at the top of the enclosure. I put the high-voltage diode, high-voltage capacitors, and discharge needle (or points) on a small piece of PC board, separate from the main circuit board (see FIG. 3-3). This made it easy to place the discharge point in a good location, relative to the fan.

If you decide to put any screen or covering on the output fan hole, I advise that it should be nonmetallic or plastic in nature. I think that using a metal screen would severely cut the efficiency of the generator because as the negative ions come into contact with the metal screen, they would be neutralized. Remember to place a few air holes in the side or bottom of your enclosure for the fan to draw air in.

3-3 An inside view of the ion generator.

If you see any arcing or discharge from the high-voltage transformer or high-voltage capacitors when testing the circuit, spray the area with a little "No Arc" spray, which is available from Radio Shack. Allow the material to dry before testing the unit again.

Parts list

TR1	120 Vac 12-V 1.2-A stepdown transformer, Radio Shack, 273-1352
BR1	4-A bridge rectifier, Radio Shack, 276-1171
C1	1000-μF capacitor, Radio Shack, 272-1032
C2	0.047-μF capacitor, Radio Shack, 272-1068
IC1	555 timer, Radio Shack, 276-1723
R1	15-kΩ 1/4-W resistor, Radio Shack, 271-1337
R2	1-kΩ 1/4-W resistor, Radio Shack, 271-1321
R3	2.2-kΩ 1/4-W resistor, Radio Shack, 271-1325
R4	470-Ω 1/4-W resistor, Radio Shack, 271-1317
Q1	TIP 120 npn Darlington, Radio Shack, 276-2068
Q2	3055 power transistor, Radio Shack, 276-2041
Fan	12-Vdc fan, Radio Shack, 276-243
TR2	High-voltage transformer, Images Co.
D1	10-kV diode, Images Co.
C3 and C4	6-kV capacitor, Images Co.
Misc	Enclosure, line cord, switch, TO-3 socket, and heatsink.

IMAGES CO.
P.O. Box 140742
Staten Island, NY 10314-0024
(718) 698-8305

Chapter 4

Bio-feedback/
lie-detector device

*B*io-feedback devices allow individuals to train or control an aspect of their autonomic physiology. *Autonomic* means automated and controlled by lower brain functions, therefore not under our conscious control. This belief is outdated; it proved to be a fallacy. Training a person to control such physiology as EEG (brain waves), EKG (heart rate), blood pressure, and tension level proved to be possible once a method became established of showing a person (feedback) the physiology changes they are trying to control in real time.

It is interesting that the control of these functions cannot be accurately taught verbally. The training or the conditioning of the body using a bio-feedback device to feel a particular way or to get a feeling controls these functions.

The types of bio-feedback devices available are numerous. The type that you will build in this chapter is a galvanic skin-resistance bio-feedback device (see FIG. 4-1). Galvanic skin resistance is a good indicator of stress level in the subject. Perhaps its most famous attribute is its use as a lie detector.

CIRCUIT DESCRIPTION

The circuit is broken down into two main parts (see FIG. 4-2). A front end consists of the op amp and resistance bridge. This is the actual bio-feedback circuit. The back end of the circuit, the 3914 IC and the 10 LEDs, make up the display section.

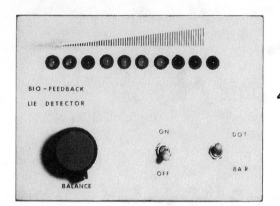

4-1 The bio-feedback unit.

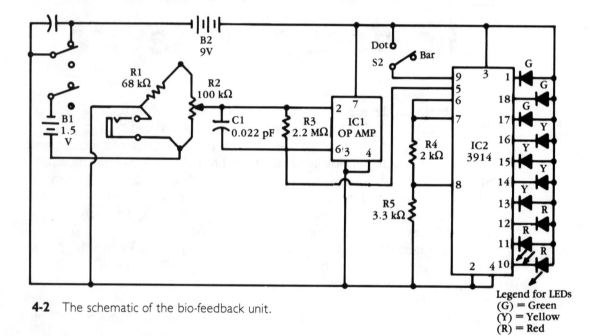

4-2 The schematic of the bio-feedback unit.

Legend for LEDs
(G) = Green
(Y) = Yellow
(R) = Red

Bio-feedback section

The advantages this galvanic-resistance device has over previous designs is that this op-amp requires a single-ended +9-V power supply in contrast to the standard 741 op amp, which requires a bipolar 9-V power supply. This really simplifies our circuit's power requirements. It does require one 1.5-V AA battery to supply power to the resistance bridge.

The circuit operation is straightforward. Looking at the schematic examine the resistance bridge that consists of the electrodes, a 1.5-V battery, 68-kΩ fixed resistor and 100-kΩ pot. When the electrodes are attached to the subject, the subject's resistance becomes part of the bridge. The bridges can be balanced using the 100-kΩ pot. The output from the bridge is fed to the input to the op amp. The op amp is set up as a difference amplifier. Once balanced, this amplifier will amplify any minor change in the subject's resistance.

The output of the op amp is directed to the input of the 3914 chip. The 3914 chip reads the voltage from the op amp and converts it into a digital display using the 10 LEDs. Bar and dot display are available from the 3914.

Electrodes

Silver is one of the best electrode materials around. You can capitalize on this by using two U.S. dimes for our electrodes. Although dimes haven't been made from pure silver for some time, they still make excellent conductors. The cable you'll use has 2 conductors with shielding. The shielding is a copper-braided wire that surrounds the 2 insulated wires in the center of the cable. Remove about 2 inches of the outer cable jacket, separate the shielding from the insulated wires. Strip 1/2 inch of insulation off of the center wires.

Soldering the wires to the dimes is a little tricky if you haven't done much soldering (see FIG. 4-3). Place the tip of your soldering iron

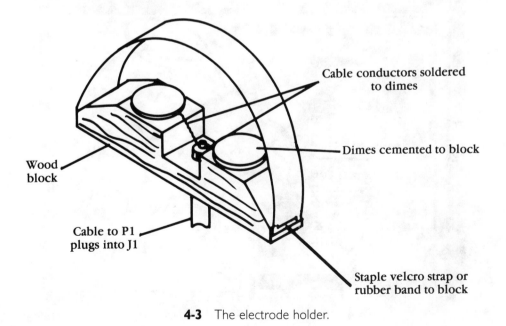

4-3 The electrode holder.

on the coin, and keep it there until the coin becomes hot enough to melt solder on it. This procedure requires about 1 to 2 minutes of continuous heating. At this point, melt a small puddle of solder on the coin, then place the bare end of one of the insulated wires into the puddle, and remove the soldering iron from the coin. Keep the wire in place until the solder solidifies. Repeat the procedure for the other coin, but solder the shielding and the wire to this coin. This will be the ground electrode.

The palm of the hand is very sensitive to galvanic changes, it is therefore the area of choice. To secure the dime electrodes to the palm of the hand, I made a small palm-fitting electrode holder out of 3/4-inch pine wood. You only need a couple of square inches of wood, so practically any piece of scrap can be used. After cutting the wood to the proper shape, drill a 1/4-inch hole through the center to feed the cable through. Then epoxy or hot glue the electrodes to the wood block. To finish the hand electrode, attach a rubber band or elastic material to the base so that it covers the electrodes. These materials will secure the holder to your hand.

Circuit construction

The circuit is fairly simple. If you look at the photograph of the circuit board (FIG. 4-4), you'll see that I used ribbon cable to connect the LEDs

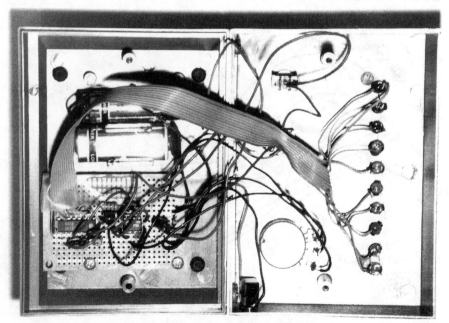

4-4 An internal view of bio-feedback unit.

to the 3914. Ribbon cable isn't necessary, but it helps to keep the LEDs in proper order. The bar/dot display-mode switch simply connects pin 9 of the 3914 to the V or lets it float.

Circuit operation

Attach the electrodes to your subject's hand by placing the wood electrode holder in their palm and the rubber band around their hand (see FIG. 4-5). Turn on the circuit, then adjust the balance pot so that the LED graph is lit approximately midway. You will notice that when adjusting the balance pot, the LEDs jump very quickly when you reach the balance area. A soft touch is required when rotating the pot around this area.

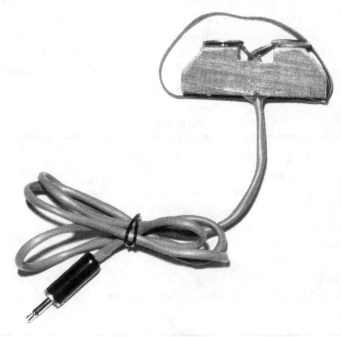

4-5 The electrode holder.

If your subject is a little nervous, you might have to adjust the balance a few times as they relax. When everything is stable, have the subject quickly inhale and exhale deeply. This should cause a rise in the LED graph, which will gradually return to the previous level. If you get this result, the circuit is operating properly and you're ready to go. If you get the opposite reaction (the LED graph dips when it should •

peak), the battery in the bridge section is reversed. In order to test the circuit, you must have some resistance connected across the electrodes or the LEDs will never light.

Bio-feedback

To use this device in a bio-feedback mode for relaxation and tension reduction, set the balance pot to light the graph in the upper portion. As you relax or reduce tension, the body's resistance increases, which will be seen as a gradual downward sloping of the graph. When you reach the bottom, you can readjust the balance pot to bring it back up and then try to bring it down again.

Lie detector

To use this device as a lie detector, set the graph on the lower portion of the graph. Any stress will cause the graph to rise. The delay between the question and response is approximately 1.5 seconds. Remember, this device is for entertainment purposes only. Even full-fledged lie detectors are fallible, and it could be the nature of the question, regardless of the answer that can cause a stress reaction.

Parts list

IC1	CMOS op amp, Images Co.
IC2	3914, Images Co.
R1	68-kΩ resistor, Radio Shack
R2	100-kΩ potentiometer, Radio Shack
R3	2.2-MΩ resistor, Radio Shack
R4 and R5	2.2-kΩ resistor, Radio Shack
C1	0.047-μF capacitor, Radio Shack
SW1	DPDT switch, Radio Shack
Misc	1.5-V battery and holder, 2 dimes for use as electrodes, case with PC board.

IMAGES CO.
P.O. Box 140742
Staten Island, NY 10314

Chapter **5**

ELF monitor

*T*here is a growing concern over possible health hazards from low-frequency electromagnetic fields. When the story first broke, the primary area of concern was the electromagnetic fields produced by overhead power-line transformers.

At the time, the reasoning was that unless you worked in the electrical/electronic fields or lived close to power lines, you could consider yourself unaffected and relatively safe. New evidence suggests that this really isn't the case. It appears that the *ELF (extremely low-frequency magnetic fields)* given off by many household appliances and computer monitors can be considered potentially hazardous.

For those of us who dabble in, or earn our livelihood in electronics or a related field, the concern becomes more prominent. This being the case, you should be aware of what research has occurred and what's been reported thus far. If, after reading the following material, you feel concerned about the issue, you can construct a simple ELF monitor to check and modify your environment. The ELF monitor is simple to build and costs less than $25.00.

WHY WASN'T IT SOONER?

The question needs to be asked, if ELF radiation does present a health hazard, why has it taken so long for anyone to uncover it? To answer this question, you must look at how scientists first interpreted potential biological hazards from low-frequency magnetic fields.

To begin with, it was originally believed that weak low-frequency fields could not have a significant impact on living systems. This belief was based on the amount of thermal energy the ELF fields could produce in biological tissue or cells. The energy transmitted is much smaller that the normal thermal energy generated internally by the cells internal metabolic processes. In addition, the quantum energy of the fields is far too low to break any chemical or nuclear bonds in the tissue. Therefore, they felt that the DNA structure was safe from mutating. Finally, the electric field of the body is much greater than any induced field from the ELF. Looking at all these factors, it's easy to understand why scientists and the scientific community in general quickly dismissed epidemiologic studies that described a statistical significant hazard associated with ELF as being flawed in one way or another.

The scientific community is not made up of a bunch of hacks, or bureaucratic puppets who are controlled by various government agencies or industrial power companies genuflecting for grants, as portrayed by the press. The reason for the quick dismissal was one of disbelief, not clandestine action for a mass cover-up. Although, in truth, a few scientists have stepped over the line and maligned good researchers, based upon the profit and loss statements of their employers. These scientists are few in number and the entire scientific community should not be condemned, based upon these isolated unethical endeavors. Most scientists, by nature of being scientists, must remain open-minded to new discoveries or should be quickly allotted a platform in a museum.

THE REAL DEAL

Although the mechanism by which ELF fields impact on biological tissue is not exactly known, it has been shown unequivocally that cellular tissue is affected. The best research data shows that the cell's membrane or receptor molecules in the membrane are sensitive to extremely weak low-frequency magnetic fields.

Some of the effects reported so far include changes in the flow of ionic compounds through the cellular membranes, changes in DNA synthesis and RNA transcription, and the response of cells to signalling molecules (such as hormones and neurotransmitters). In addition, changes have been noted in the kinetics of some cellular biochemical reactions.

Not all ELF produces all these effects, it's more complex than that. Some effects are noted at the discrete frequency and amplitude of the field. Others depend on the strength and orientation of an ambient dc magnetic field. Still others require a threshold that is determined more by exposure time than field strength.

It has been emphasized in the press the inherent danger or increased likelihood of various forms of cancer with exposure to ELF. As stated previously, the quantum energy of these fields isn't sufficient to produce any type of chromosomal damage. Simply, the ELF doesn't initiate cancer. The association to the increased incidence of cancers involves its promotion after the cancer has been triggered by another agent. The promotion of cancer is caused by the ELF suppression on the body's immune system (see cell response to ELF above). In addition, at the cellular level, it has been determined that the ELF fields increase the production of the enzyme ornithine decarboxylase, which has been cited to support the promotion of cancer in the body.

THE EVIDENCE

As studies progress, more information will be forthcoming. Here is a short list of reported events that indicates the potential health hazards of ELF fields.

- 1972. Soviet researchers link electromagnetic fields with low-grade health problems, such as fatigue and headaches.

- 1977. Robert Becker, physician, and Andrew Marino, biophysicist, testified before the N.Y.S. Public Service Commission about the results of their experiments, which showed negative health effects as a result of exposure to ELF fields.

- 1979. Nancy Wertheimer, epidemiologist, and Ed Leeper, physicist, published a study, which showed statistical link between childhood cancers and the proximity of certain types of high-current power lines to the home.

- 1982. A Washington state study examined the data for 438,000 deaths of workers in Washington state, occurring between 1950 and 1979. The results of the study found that leukemia deaths were elevated in 10 out of 11 occupations where the workers were exposed to ELF fields.

- 1986. Dr. Bernard Tribukait, a professor of radiobiology at the Karolinska Institute in Stockholm, Sweden, reported that the fetuses of mice exposed to sawtooth-shaped electromagnetic pulsed fields had a greater incident of congenital malformation than unexposed mice. The sawtooth waveform is a typical waveform generated in CRT monitors.

- 1988. The Maryland Department of Health and Hygiene found an unusually high rate of fatal brain cancer among men who were employed in electrical occupations.

- 1989. John Hopkins University found an elevated risk of all cancers among N.Y. Telephone Co. cable splicers. An on-site reading of the ELF field showed that the exposure to 60-Hz ELF was approximately 4.3 milligauss.

- 1990. David Savitz, epidemiologist of the University of North Carolina, determined through a study that pregnant women who used an electric blanket had children with a 30% increased risk of cancer, as compared to children whose mother didn't use an electric blanket.

Not all the news is bad

So far, I have concentrated on the negative effects of the 60-Hz ELF fields. You should know that there are positive medical uses for ELF fields. Robert Becker had discovered that ELF fields, when appropriately applied (specific frequency and amplitude), can promote healing and therapeutic responses in tissue (see Dr. Becker under 1977 evidence). The ELF fields appear to be a double-edge sword: they can heal as well as injure.

Computer monitors

Concern over televisions and computer monitors (which are closely related in operation and technology) is nothing new. A number of years ago, there was a concern about whether radiation given off by color televisions could have a negative impact on health. This concern was based primarily on ionizing radiation (low-level X-rays), whose intensity fell off dramatically a few inches away from the TV screen, and turned out to be incidental. More insidious than this overt obvious threat is one that has passed unnoticed until quite recently: the low-frequency magnetic fields generated by the electromagnets used on the CRT (cathode-ray tube) screen.

Computer monitors generate these low-frequency magnetic fields, which emanate in all directions from its position. More important to us is how close we keep ourselves to the monitor to read the screen and use the computer. Here is a concern.

Excessive ELF fields emitted by computer monitors is an industry-wide problem. Virtually all CRT computer monitors emit excessive ELF, unless specifically stated otherwise. Recently, *MacWorld Magazine* (7/

90 issue) did ELF studies on 10 popular computer monitors. All of the monitors tested emitted excessive ELF at close range. The only recommendation that they or I can offer at this time is to increase the distance between you and the monitor. A working distance of two feet is recommended. Below are the results I obtained when I checked the ELF output of one computer monitor that I use in my home.

Tale of the tape

The ELF field propagates from all points around the monitor, not just from the front screen. This fact becomes important in offices where computer terminals are in close to one another. Operators can be exposed not only from their own monitor but also from a neighbor's monitor.

It's important to realize that the ELF field will vary somewhat from monitor to monitor. These are the measurements of the 60-Hz ELF field that I read from my 1084 Amiga monitor. My readings are given in milligauss. Magnetic field strength is measured in gauss, but this unit of measure is too large for our purposes. Thus, I used 1 milligauss, which is $1/1000$ of a gauss.

Distance	Front	L-Side	R-Side	Back	Top	Bottom
0"	78	97	90	125	270	N/C
4"	24	14	16	37	65	N/C
12"	5	1.5	1.5	8	9	N/C
24"	<1	<1	<1	3	1.5	N/C

As you can see, the ELF strength drops off dramatically with distance from the monitor. I could not check the ELF radiating from the bottom of the monitor because of the way it is situated in my work space.

Shielding

It would be nice if we could purchase a shield for our monitors, similar to the anti-glare shield on the market. Unfortunately, none exist. Be very careful, some anti-glare screens on the market make a claim to block the electric and magnetic fields given off from the monitor. First, electric fields as far as I know have not been reported to have any negative impact upon health. Second, the magnetic field these screens claim to block are, in fact, the high-frequency fields generated by the CRT. These high-frequency magnetic fields have not been shown to have a negative impact on health. These screens have no impact on the low-frequency (60 Hz) magnetic fields that I am talking about.

There is no easy way to shield the monitor to reduce the propagating ELF field. I have tried a number of different methods, none had any appreciable impact on the ELF. The best recommendation is to keep the monitor 18 to 24 inches away from yourself.

Another possibility is to use an alternative-type computer monitor. LCD (liquid-crystal display) and plasma display screens do not emit ELF fields. The drawbacks are a higher cost and lower resolution.

Precautions around the home

Other sources of ELF exist around the typical home. An appliance in the home might generate a very strong ELF field, but if the appliance is only used a short time, its risk factor is probably low. Notice the word *probably* in the last sentence. Currently, exact data on short-term high-strength fields hasn't been gathered. Electric razors fall into this category. Line-operated (plugged into a wall socket, rather than battery powered) razors do produce extremely strong ELF fields, and are held very close to the body, but because they are only used a short time, the total exposure or dose is small and they are probably safe.

In contrast to the electric razor is the electric blanket. These blankets have a much lower ELF field strength, but a much longer exposure. Dr. Nancy Wertheimer, who first published the epidemiological study that showed a correlation between 60-Hz power lines and an increased incidence of childhood cancer in this country, has also performed similar research on users of electric blankets. She has found a higher incidence of miscarriage among pregnant women who use electric blankets, as compared to pregnant women who do not.

For users of electric blankets, the following recommendations can be made. One, switch to ordinary blankets. If you like electric blankets, use it to heat your bed before going to sleep, but unplug the blanket before you actually get into bed. It is not sufficient to just turn off the blanket because many blankets still produce the ELF field as long as its plugged into the socket. The AMA has gone one step further by recommending that the electric blanket be removed entirely. They have found that the blanket acts like an antenna for ELF radiation.

It's impossible for me to state what a safe long-term dose rate is because it hasn't been established. Effects have been reported at dose rates as low as 1.2 to 3 milligauss. So, I would venture to say to try to limit long-term exposure of ELF to 1 milligauss or less.

Television   Television sets fall into the same category as our computer monitors. Like our monitors, they produce a field that propagates around the entire set. The ELF field will propagate through standard building materials, such as wood and plaster. So, if a TV set is placed against a wall, the ELF will propagate through into the adjoining room. So, it becomes important not to place a bed against an adjoining wall that is opposite a TV set.

VDT   *VDT* represents *video display terminal*, a computer monitor. There have been numerous reports from female computer operators of cluster miscarriages. The word *cluster* refers to a greater than average incident of miscarriages among a group of women. The latest study on cluster miscarriages was performed in 1988 by doctors Marilyn Goldhaber, Micheal Polen, and Robert Hiat of the Kaiser Permanente Health Group in Oakland, California. The study involved 1,583 pregnant women. The results of the study showed that female workers who used computers more than 20 hours per week had double the miscarriage rate, as compared to female workers who did similar work without computers.

What this study didn't take into account (but which I am sure will be studied in the near future) is the incident of malformations and cancers in the children born to the women who used the computers, as compared to the children of the women who didn't. If we extrapolate the information from the David Savitz 1990 study, you might see another side to the problem.

Fluorescent lights   Fluorescent lights are much more efficient (more light per electrical watt) than ordinary incandescent bulbs. Because of this, fluorescent lighting has become the standard lighting system used for most commercial office and industrial lighting. However, fluorescent lights require a ballast transformer, which generates an ELF field. If you're using a small fluorescent lamp as a desk light, you might want to consider switching to an incandescent lamp, which generates virtually no ELF.

This also applies to the new energy-saver fluorescent lamps that replace standard incandescent bulbs. These are alright for overhead lighting, but you might want to reconsider using them for close-up work or desk lighting.

Electric clocks   Small electric clocks that are plugged into a wall socket also produces an ELF field from the small internal electric motor. If an alarm clock lies close to the sleeper's head, it could be giving a significant ELF dose during the night time. The recommendations would be to move the clock a significant distance away or to purchase either a battery-powered clock or a digital clock that produces a negligible field.

Hair dryers   Hair dryers fall in the same category as electric shavers: short term, high field-strength exposure. These are probably safe for most people. Notable exceptions are people who use these in their occupation: hair stylists and hair dressers.

Electric heaters   Electric baseboard heaters are another potential problem appliance. The recommendation is a minimum of 4 feet from heater for furniture, such as beds.

Bottom line   A controversy still rages as to the impact and extent of ELF fields on human health. I feel there is sufficient evidence for us to take a conservative view on the amount of exposure we should allow ourselves to be exposed to, especially because you are probably in the electronics field. I would try to limit long-term exposure to one milliguass or less. Of course, it's difficult to know what your ELF exposure level is without a milligaussmeter (a device used to measure ELF). The ELF monitor that you can build measures the 60-Hz magnetic field from any appliance. The resolution (trip point) of the meter is about 1.5 to 2.5 milliguass. By using the meter around your home, apartment, or work space, you can identify potentially hazardous ELF fields and the sources for you to implement corrective action. If you decided not to build the meter, I'd advise you to follow the precautions outlined above; they will help to reduce your ELF exposure.

ELF MONITOR

The heart of this project is the ELF monitor (see FIG. 5-1). The sensor detects the 60-Hz field and outputs a voltage in proportion to the magnetic field strength. The sensor is a Radio Shack telephone pick-up coil. This simple sensor doesn't have the resolution of the more expensive sensors, but it is sufficient to build a simple low-cost go/no-go ELF monitor.

The circuit uses a Dual-BIFET op amp (see FIG. 5-2). A germanium diode in the feedback loop provides nonlinear feedback. The diode allows the op amp to amplify and rectify millivolt signals from the sensor. When there is insufficient output voltage from the op amp to drive the diode into conduction, the feedback is open and the op amp operates at its full voltage gain. At this point only, a small voltage from the ELF sensor is required to produce a large output. In doing so, it drives

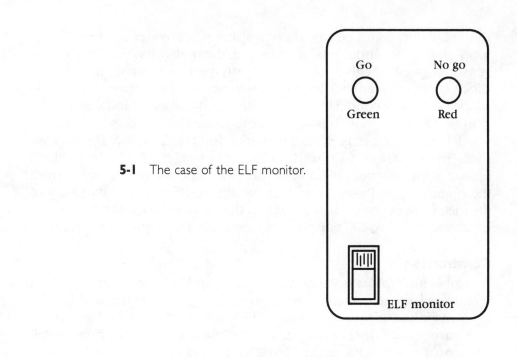

5-1 The case of the ELF monitor.

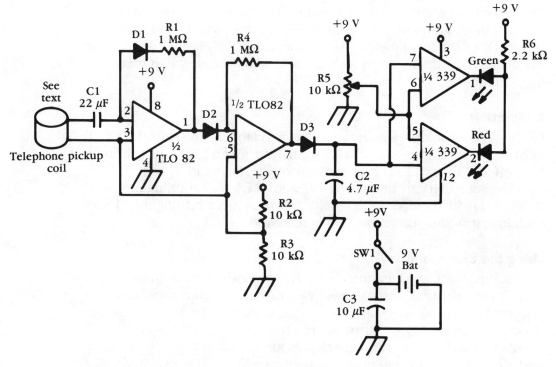

5-2 The schematic of the ELF monitor.

diode D1 into conduction, where resistor R1 provides a lower closed-loop gain of the input signal. In practice, the millivolt ac signal from the sensor is put through a half-wave rectifying op-amp amplifier, where diode D1 in the feedback loop compensates for the voltage drop across diode D2. The second half of the op amp provides additional amplification of the signal, which is sufficient to drive the 339 display chip.

I choose to use germanium diodes for D1, D2, and D3 because these have a lower voltage drop (approximately 0.3 V) than silicon diodes (approximately 0.7 V) and provide superior performance from the op amp. The PC-mounted potentiometer, R5, allows calibration of the meter. Capacitor C1 is provided on the input to block any dc component. A simple two-LED display is made from a 339 quad comparator.

Construction

Assemble and solder components on a small PC board. Keep the lead lengths as short as possible to minimize stray pickup in the wiring. The ELF sensor has shielded wire protruding from the side. Cut this wire off and leave about 3 inches on the sensor. Split and strip the wires. Install the sensor to the front of the plastic case using epoxy or hot glue. The top of the case is drilled for the two LEDs and the power switch. Power for the circuit is supplied by a single 9-V battery, which is mounted on the inside of the front panel. Use a nonconductive plastic case, such as the one in the parts list from Radio Shack. A metal case will impede any measurements.

Calibration

Calibration must occur in an area that is relatively free of 60-Hz ELF. Turn on the monitor and adjust R5 so that the green LED is just about to turn off and the red LED is about to turn on. That's it!

The sensitivity of the monitor is about 1.5 to 2.5 milliguass. The monitor quickly detects an ELF field, however it is a bit sluggish (1 second) in responding once the field is removed.

Using the ELF monitor

The ELF monitor will measure the 60-Hz magnetic field from any appliance. To test the unit, turn on a television, starting from approximately 2 feet away, and slowly walk the sensor closer to the set. As you get closer, the green LED will turn off and the red LED will turn on.

As you walk around and check various appliances, you'll probably find that by rearrangement you can lower your ELF exposure. For instance, one of my computers has an external power supply that emitted strong ELF. I simply moved the power supply further away from my work space to a more discrete location. Other simple things include changing from a fluorescent desk lamp to an incandescent desk lamp.

The ELF monitor can also detect a static magnetic field, when it is moved into or out of the field. If the monitor remains fixed in the magnetic field for a short time, the green LED will come back on.

Parts list

Sensor	Telephone pick-up coil, Radio Shack, 44-533B
IC1	Dual BIFET op amp, Radio Shack, 276-1715
IC2	339 quad comparator, Radio Shack, 276-1712
S1	On/off switch, Radio Shack, 275-690
C1	0.22-μF capacitor, Radio Shack, 272-1070
C2	4.7-μF capacitor, Radio Shack, 272-1012
D1, D2, D3	IN34A diode, Radio Shack, 276-1123
R1, R4	1-MΩ 1/4-W resistor, Radio Shack
R2, R3	10-kΩ 1/4-W resistor, Radio Shack
R5	10-kΩ PCB-mount resistor, Radio Shack, 271-282
R6	2.2-kΩ 1/4-W resistor, Radio Shack
LED	Red (276-041) and green 276-022, Radio Shack
SW1	SPST, Radio Shack, 275-634, Radio Shack
Case	Plastic, Radio Shack, 270-233
Misc.	9-V battery, clip, and holder; LED holders; and PC breadboard.

Chapter **6**

Hydrophone

*A*quatic sea life produces sounds as diverse and intriguing as those of land animals. Although a few audio cassettes are available of recorded whale songs and dolphin sounds, for the most part these underwater sounds are left unheard.

Scuba divers, I am told, hear a few muffled underwater sounds. I have never heard any aquatic life on any of my dives. For the most part, to hear underwater sounds accurately, we need a *hydrophone*. A hydrophone is designed to receive underwater vibrations and convert them into weak electrical signals. Essentially, a hydrophone is an underwater microphone. The weak electrical signals can be amplified, as with a standard microphone, and listened to from a loudspeaker.

The most obvious use for the hydrophone is to listen to fish and other aquatic life, such as whales and dolphins. Other applications range from a turbulence monitor to listen for boat and ship propellers to a splash monitor for swimming pools.

Fortunately for this project, you do not have to construct the hydrophone itself, they are available from Edmund Scientific, see the index of suppliers. In this chapter, you can construct a suitable audio amplifier. By connecting the hydrophone to this amplifier, you can listen in on underwater sounds.

HYDROPHONE SPECIFICATIONS

The hydrophone (see FIG. 6-1) can be used in either fresh or salt water. It has an operating depth of 300 feet. The frequency response of the

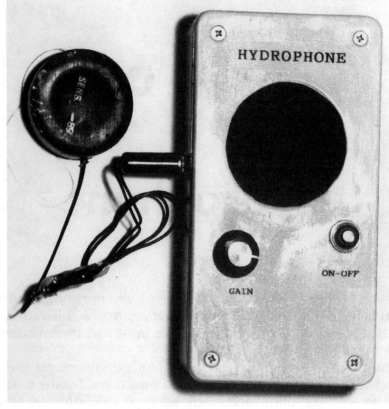

6-1 The hydrophone.

hydrophone is 10 to 6000 Hz. The roll off is greater than 12 dB per octave above 7000 Hz. This frequency response is fine as most aquatic life produces sound in the low frequencies.

AUDIO AMPLIFIER

The amplifier for the hydrophone is made with four IC modules (see FIG. 6-2). The signal from the hydrophone is preamplified by IC1, configured as a 15X amplifier. The amplified signal passes through IC2 (a 60-Hz notch filter) and IC3 (a low-pass filter with a 7000-Hz frequency cutoff). The filtered signal is amplified by IC4, an LM386 audio amplifier to the speaker SPK1. Potentiometer R12 controls the gain of the LM386 amplifier. All of these parts are available at Radio Shack, and the Radio Shack part numbers are included in the parts list.

The construction is not critical. The most difficult part is securing the speaker to the housing. I placed speaker cloth and the speaker on

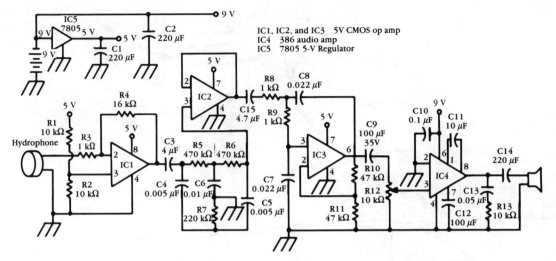

6-2 The schematic of the hydrophone.

the opening in the housing and used hot glue to secure everything. If you don't have a hot glue gun, I'm sure epoxy will work just as well.

The hydrophone comes with attached leads that are connected with shielded cable to a 1/8-inch phono plug. The wire coming out of the hydrophone is thin. Carefully strip away the insulation and separate the wires. Solder one wire from the hydrophone to the shield of the cable; this should be the ground on the phono plug. When the wires are soldered, secure the connections with electrical tape. Then, water-proof the connection with silicone rubber sealant, available from a tropical fish store to fix leaks in aquariums.

USE

To test the unit, turn the volume control (R12) for maximum gain. Pass your finger across the surface of the hydrophone. You should hear a loud scraping sound from the speaker.

The hydrophone can be mounted various ways, depending on the use. It can be mounted on a handle, pole, or secondary cable line. Do not support the hydrophone by its electrical wire. Instead, use a sec-ondary cable. Wrap the cable around the hydrophone. Secure the cable to the hydrophone with a hose clamp. Wrap or tape the audio wire to the secondary cable line. Make sure that stress is placed on the second-ary cable and not on the electrical wires. Figure 6-3 shows how this setup can be used off a boat.

You can also use the hydrophone to listen in to home aquariums.

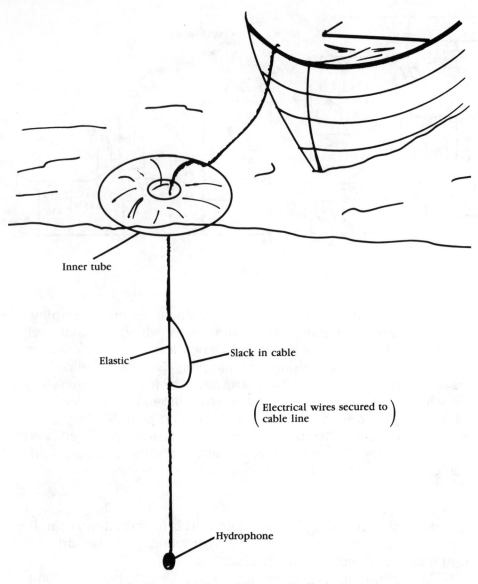

6-3 The hydrophone being used off of a boat.

Not all aquatic animals make sounds, but you will need to turn off the filter and the air pumps to keep from drowning out all sounds in order to hear anything.

Parts list

Hydrophone	Edmund Scientific, C41-759
IC1, IC2, IC3	5-V CMOS op amp, Images Co.
IC4	LM386 audio amp, Radio Shack, 276-1731
IC5	7805 voltage regulator, Radio Shack, 276-1770
R1, R2	10-kΩ resistor, Radio Shack, 271-034
R3, R8, R9	1-kΩ resistor, Radio Shack, 271-023
R4	15-kΩ resistor, Radio Shack, 271-036
R5, R6	470-kΩ resistor, Radio Shack, 271-053
R7	220-kΩ resistor, Radio Shack, 271-049
R10, R11	47-kΩ resistor, Radio Shack, 271-042
R13	10-Ω resistor, Radio Shack, 271-001
R12	10-kΩ potentiometer, Radio Shack, 271-1715
C1, C2, C14	220-μF capacitor, Radio Shack, 271-1029
C3	47-μF capacitor, Radio Shack, 272-1027
C4, C5	0.0047-μF capacitor, Radio Shack, 272-130
C6	0.01-μF capacitor, Radio Shack, 272-1065
C7, C8	0.022-μF capacitor, Radio Shack, 272-1066
C9, C12	100-μF capacitor, Radio Shack, 272-1028
C10	0.1-μF capacitor, Radio Shack, 272-1432
C11	10-μF capacitor, Radio Shack, 272-1025
C13	0.047-μF capacitor, Radio Shack, 272-1068
C15	4.7-μF capacitor, Radio Shack, 272-1024
SPK1	2$1/4$-inch speaker, Radio Shack, 40-246
Misc.	Housing, 9-V battery, cap and holder, knob, PC board, shielded cable, 1/8-inch phono plug and jacket.

EDMUND SCIENTIFIC
101 E. Gloucester Pike
Barrington, NJ 08007-1380
(609) 573-6250

IMAGES COMPANY
P.O. Box 140742
Staten Island, NY 10314-0024
(718) 698-8305

Chapter **7**

Geiger counter project

We are surrounded by energy that we cannot observe with our senses. For instance, turn on a radio and you can listen to broadcasted electromagnetic signals that have been passing through you and your home completely unnoticed. You are not aware of this electromagnetic radiation directly because you can't see, hear, feel or taste it with any of your senses. The same is true of radioactivity. To detect radioactivity, you can build a Geiger counter, which will give visual and audible indications of local radioactivity.

RADIOACTIVITY

Simply put, *radioactivity* is the spontaneous emission of energy from the atomic nucleus of certain elements. The energy emitted can take the form of particles (as in alpha and beta particles) or electromagnetic energy (as in gamma rays).

In general, people are concerned with radioactivity in the form of ionizing radiation. This is because of its relationship to atomic weapons and nuclear power plants. There is also a legitimate concern over long-lived waste products from nuclear power plants and their potential for ecological damage.

Background radiation

Perhaps radioactivity can be put into a better perspective by looking at some natural sources of radioactivity. To begin with, life on this planet has always been exposed to an environment in which cosmic rays, naturally occurring radioactive materials in the soil (uranium-238 and thorium-232), and food (potassium-40 and carbon-14) maintain a continuous background level of radiation. In essence, we live in this radioactive environment, where millions of gamma rays pass through each individual on Earth every hour.

The background radiation will cause the Geiger counter to click about 12 to 14 times per minute. This is normal. As stated, millions of gamma rays penetrate every one of us every hour, so naturally not all the radiation passing through the GM tube is detected.

The Geiger counter that you will construct can be used to detect nuclear radiation or contamination in your home or local area, prospect for uranium, measure the background radiation, and sometimes even detect solar flares.

History

Radioactivity was discovered in 1896 by French scientist Henri Becquerel. He found that pitchblende ore (which contains uranium-238) fogged photographic plates—even though the plates were kept completely covered and unexposed to light. Today, we know that this radiation consisted of alpha (α) particles. The two other types of radiation emitted from radioactive materials: beta (β) and gamma (Γ). The term *radioactivity* was coined by Pierre and Marie Curie to name this phenomenon. They also proved that radioactivity is an atomic property and not a chemical one.

Alpha particles are helium-4 nucleus, which consist of two protons and two neutrons. When an atomic nucleus emits an alpha particle, it obviously changes into another nuclide with an atomic number of two units less and a mass number of four units less. For instance, when uranium-238 emits an alpha particle, it transmutes to thorium-234. Alpha particles do not penetrate very far. They can be stopped by a few sheets of paper or a few inches of air.

Beta particles are either electrons or positrons (positive electrons). Beta particles are more penetrating than alpha particles, but they can be stopped by thin metal sheets (such as aluminum foil) or a few feet of air.

Gamma rays have deep penetration; they can go through several inches of lead. Gamma rays are photons of energy (quanta) emitted from excited atoms. They are not associated with any particle. When an atom, such as uranium-238, emits an alpha particle, it becomes thorium-234. The thorium atom, at this point, has excess energy. It is said to be in an excited state and by emitting a gamma ray, it drops to its ground state (unexcited).

Measurement of radioactivity

A number of ways are available to measure radioactivity, such as scintillation, gas ionization, pn junctions, and auto radiography. The Geiger-Muller tube works on the gas-ionization principle. Surprisingly, the Geiger-Muller tube of today looks pretty much the same as the original tube, except that it is miniaturized. The GM tube in this project detects alpha, beta, and gamma rays.

In 1920, it was decided that the amount of radiation given off by one gram of radium be named *the curie*, in honor of the discoverers of radium. This unit of measure is equal to 37,000,000,000 (3.7×10^{10}) atomic breakdowns per second. The curie is a rather large number and many radioactive sources are measures in millicuries ($1/1000$ of a curie) or microcuries (1×10^{-6} of a curie). A microcurie (μci) is equal to 3.7×10^4 or 37,000 breakdowns per second.

Geiger tube Figure 7-1 shows the basic operating principle of the Geiger-Muller (GM) tube. The tube is constructed with a cylindrical electrode (cathode) surrounding a center electrode (anode). The tube is evacuated and filled with a neon and halogen gas mixture. A voltage potential of 500 V is applied across the tube, through 10-MΩ current-limiting resistor R1. The detection of radiation relies on its ability to ionize the gas in the GM tube. The tube has an extremely high resistance when it is not in the process of detecting radioactivity. When an atom of the gas is ionized by the passage of radiation, the free electron and the positive-ionized atom that was created move rapidly toward the two electrodes in the GM tube. In doing so, they collide with other atoms, which also ionize and create a small avalanche effect. This ionization drops the resistance of the tube, and allows a sudden surge of electric current that creates a voltage across resistor R2. You can see this voltage as a pulse. The halogen gas quickly quenches the ionization, thus returning the GM tube to its high initial resistance and its ability to detect another particle.

The number of pulses per minute that the GM tube responds to rises with the voltage potential across its electrodes. By increasing the voltage, it reaches a plateau where the count rate stays pretty constant. The plateau range for this GM tube lies between 400 and 600 V, and the recommended operating voltage is 500 V. If you apply too much voltage to the tube, it might damage it. In this case, when the tube detects a

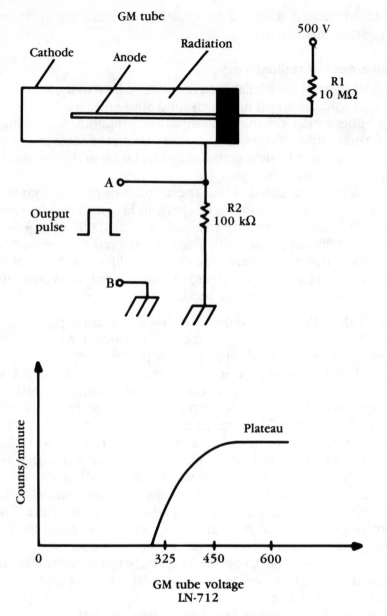

7-1 The GM tube and operation chart.

radioactive particle and the voltage is too high, the avalanche created
will not be quenched; the tube will remain in a state of continuous discharge, which can damage the tube.

THE CIRCUIT

The circuit is shown in FIG. 7-2. IC2 is a 555 timer set in the astable mode. The signal from IC2 is presented to three gates on the 4049 (IC1). The 4049 inverts the signal to give an optimum pulse width that switches Q1 on and off. The MOSFET (Q1) in turn switches the current to step-up transformer TR1. The stepped-up voltage from TR1 first passes through a voltage doubler; the output voltage from this section is approximately 600 to 700 V. Three zener diodes (D3, D4, and D5— note the polarity) are placed across the output of the voltage doubler to clamp and regulate the voltage to 500 V. The 500-V+ voltage is connected to the anode on the GM tube through a 10-MΩ resistor. The resistor limits the current through the GM tube and allows the detection ionization to be quenched. On the cathode side of the tube is a 100-kΩ resistor, which is connected to ground.

When the GM tube detects a particle, a voltage pulse from the 100-kΩ resistor is amplified and clamped to Vcc via Q2, an npn Darlington transistor. The signal from Q2 is inverted by a gate on IC1, where it acts as a trigger signal to IC3. IC3 is another 555 timer configured to the

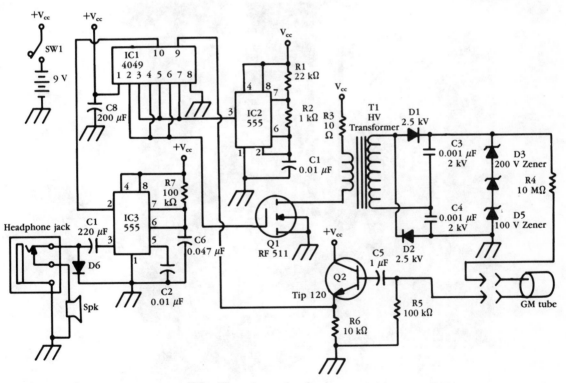

7-2 The schematic of geiger counter.

monostable mode, which stretches each pulse received. The output of IC3 via pin 3 flashes the LED and provides a click into either the speaker or the headphones. The circuit is powered by a 9-V alkaline battery and draws about 28 mA when not detecting.

Construction

Nothing is critical with this circuit; it can be handwired (see FIG. 7-3). However, you should be careful of the +500-V high-voltage that is created by the circuit. Although the current is very low, it is still capable of shocking you if you're not careful.

To make construction much easier, make a PC board for the project. Any plastic enclosure large enough to hold the circuit board and other components is fine.

The GM tube is delicate and should be handled carefully. On the front end of the tube is a thin mica window, which allows alpha and beta rays to penetrate and be detected. Be careful because this window

7-3 The inside view geiger counter.

7-4 The geiger counter.

is easy to break and would render the tube useless. It's a good idea to enclose the GM tube in its own housing (see FIG. 7-4). A microphone case is an excellent housing. Radio Shack sells an inexpensive microphone for $4.95 that looks as though it will work. Instead, I used a plastic coin tube for my GM-tube housing. I cushioned the tube with soft foam rubber around the diameter (see FIG. 7-5). I circle-cut some foam at the diameter of the tube and stuffed it into the plastic tube to take up the dead space at the bottom. If you use conductive foam, do not allow the foam to touch both electrodes on the GM tube. This will put a short across the GM tube and render the unit inoperative.

On the top cover of the tube, I drilled a number of small holes to allow alpha and beta particles through to the mica window unimpeded. I soldered about three feet of two-conductor shielded wire to the bottom leads of the tube. It is threaded through a drilled hole in the bottom of the coin tube. At the opposite end of the shielded wire, I soldered a 1/8-inch plug that connects the tube to the main circuit. This plug allows you to remove the GM tube from the case for storage. I also

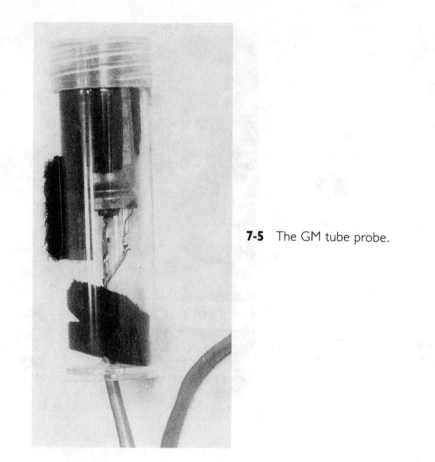

7-5 The GM tube probe.

secured a small amount of velcro to the side of the case and coin tube to secure the GM housing to the case.

Radioactive sources

A reliable source of low-level radioactive materials is the Nucleus Company (see the parts list). This company sells calibrated and uncalibrated radioactive sources for students, schools, and industries. I have purchased a cesium-137 gamma-ray source for $25.00. This material is rated at 5 μci with a 30-year half life. It was pretty enlightening to place a $3/4$-inch solid block of aluminum in front of the cesium-137, and find no noticeable decrease in radiation.

Checking and troubleshooting

Before plugging in the GM tube, it's a good idea to see if the circuit is functioning properly. Turn on the circuit. You should be able to measure approximately 500 V+ from the junction of D3 and C3, with respect to ground. If you're not getting a proper reading, first check the zener diodes to make sure that you have them facing the right direction. Next, check pin 3 of IC2; you should read a 5000-Hz square-wave pulse. Trace this pulse through IC1, which inverts this signal going to Q1. Q1 powers the step-up transformer TR1. The output of TR1 is connected to a voltage doubler, which is regulated by the zener diodes. This is the main power supply for the GM tube.

When the circuit checks out, turn it off and plug in the GM tube. Then, turn it on again. In my area, I read approximately eleven pulses per minute from the background radiation. As each particle is detected, the speaker will click and the LED will flash. If you have acquired some radioactive material, bring the GM tube close to it to test for activity.

Other Geiger tubes

The circuit is designed around the LN-712 Geiger tube. It is possible to use other Geiger tubes. The power supply can power any tube up to about 700 V. You can change the voltage output of the circuit by changing or removing the zener diodes across the output. By doing so, you can vary the voltage output up or down.

If, for instance, you have a tube that requires 350 V, simply remove one of the 200-V zener diodes, use a jumper wire between the two open terminals, and you have a regulated 350-V supply. If you need 600 V, switch out the 100-V zener diode with a 200-V zener and you have a regulated 600-V supply. Other tubes might require a different current-limiting resistor. This becomes a simple matter of removing R4 and replacing it with the proper current-limiting resistor for that particular tube.

Inverse square law

All radiation follows *the inverse square law*, which states that the intensity of the radiation is proportional to the square of the distance from its source. Put another way, if the distance from the source is 2, the intensity is $1/4$ (if the distance is 3, the intensity is $1/9$) of the intensity of the radiation at a distance of 1. What this means for our small radiation sources is that the intensity falls off pretty dramatically with distance.

Radiation will deviate (greater losses) from the inverse square law as a result of air absorption and scattering (alpha and beta particles). Another factor that weighs heavily is the area of the detector that is exposed to the radiation (gamma rays).

Detecting solar flares

As stated previously, part of the natural background radiation on Earth is caused by cosmic rays. The origin of cosmic rays can be galactic, entering our solar system from all directions, or they might be solar cosmic rays, emitting from the Sun.

The energy emitted from the Sun is more or less continuous. However, when a solar flare occurs, there is a rapid eruption of x-ray and UV energy from 10 to 100 times the normal level. This burst of energy can be detected on Earth with a simple GM counter. To do this experiment, make prolonged recordings and subtract the background radiation from the readings. This will identify bursts of radioactivity that can be correlated to current solar activity (see NOAA).

Parts list

IC1	4049 hex buffer, Radio Shack, 276-2449
IC2 and IC3	555 timer, Radio Shack, 276-1723
Q1	IRF511 MOSFET, Radio Shack, 276-2072
Q2	TIP-120 npn, Radio Shack, 276-2068
R1	22-kΩ resistor, Radio Shack, 271-1339
R2	1-kΩ resistor, Radio Shack, 271-1321
R3	10-Ω resistor, Radio Shack, 271-1301
R4	10-MΩ resistor, Radio Shack, 271-1365
R5 and R7	100-kΩ resistor Radio Shack, 271-1347
R6	10-kΩ resistor, Radio Shack, 271-1335
C1 and C2	0.01-μF capacitor, Radio Shack, 272-1065
C3 and C4	0.01-μF 2-kV capacitor, Radio Shack, 272-160
C5	1-μF capacitor, Radio Shack, 272-996
C6	0.047-μF capacitor, Radio Shack, 272-1068
C7 and C8	220-μF capacitor, Radio Shack, 276-956
D1 and D2	1-kV diode, Radio Shack, 276-1114
D3 and D4	1N5388B 200-V zener diode, Images Co.
D5	1N5271B 100-V zener diode, Images Co.
D6	Red LED, Radio Shack, 276-044
Spk	8-Ω 2.25-inch speaker, Radio Shack, 40-246
GM Tube	LN-712 GM tube, Images Co.
PC board	PCB-GM1, Images Co.
TR1	C-2B transformer, Allegro Electronics

THE NUCLEUS COMPANY
601 Oak Ridge Turnpike
Oak Ridge, TN 37830
(615) 483-8405
(800) 255-1978

IMAGES COMPANY
P.O. Box 1407423
Staten Island, NY 10314-0024
(718) 698-8305

ALLEGRO ELECTRONICS
Mine Mountain Rd.
Cornwall Bridge, CT 06754
(203) 672-0123

Chapter **8**

MHD generator

A *magnetohydrodynamic (MHD) generator* produces electrical power. As in a conventional generator, it produces power by moving a conductor through a magnetic field. The moving conductor in a standard generator is a coil of copper wire. Unlike a standard electrical generator, the MHD contains no moving parts. In the MHD, the conductor is a fast-moving hot plasma gas.

MHD BASICS

Figure 8-1 illustrates the basic operation of the MHD generator. The high-temperature, electrically conductive gas flows past a transverse magnetic field. An electric field is generated perpendicular to the direction of gas flow and the magnetic field. The electric field generated is directly proportional to the speed of the flowing gas, its electrical conductivity, and the magnetic flux density. Electricity can be siphoned off with electrodes placed in contact with the flowing plasma gas. MHD generators require a strong magnetic field. In order to make MHD generators a practical energy supply, superconductive magnets must be used.

Making a plasma

The plasma in the MHD is created by a process called *thermal ionization*. The temperature of the gas is raised to the point where the elec-

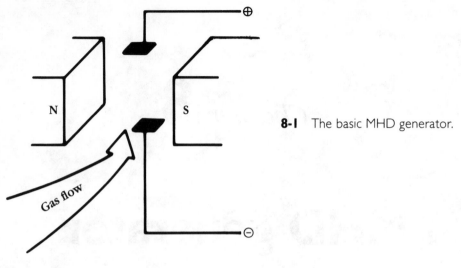

8-1 The basic MHD generator.

trons are no longer bound to the atoms of gas. These free electrons make the plasma gas electrically conductive.

To create such a plasma through thermal ionization alone requires extraordinarily high temperatures. The gas temperature can be lowered significantly by seeding the gas with an alkali metal, such as potassium nitrate. The alkali metal ionizes easily at lower temperatures.

In this model, the gas is continuously seeded with potassium nitrate, which makes the gas electrically conductive at lower temperatures.

Advantages of MHD generators

Conventional coal-fired generators achieve a maximum efficiency of about 35%. MHD generators have the potential to reach 50% or 60% efficiency. The higher efficiency is caused by recycling the energy from the hot plasma gas to standard steam turbines. After the plasma gas passes through the MHD generator, it is still hot enough to boil water to drive steam turbines, which produces additional power.

MHD generators are also ecologically sound. Coal with a high sulfur content can be used in the MHD without polluting the atmosphere.

MHD MODEL

The table-top model MHD generator is pretty easy to build. Numerous heat and conductivity losses are caused by its simple construction. You should look at this as an opportunity to vastly improve on its design and, consequently, its power output. Be cautious at all times because the MHD generator is a bad burn hazard.

Figure 8-2 illustrates the construction. Two large ceramic magnets are self-supported, using three steel plates (see the parts list). The self-supporting magnets form a chamber where the electrodes are positioned. A small baseboard supports six wire electrodes. The electrode

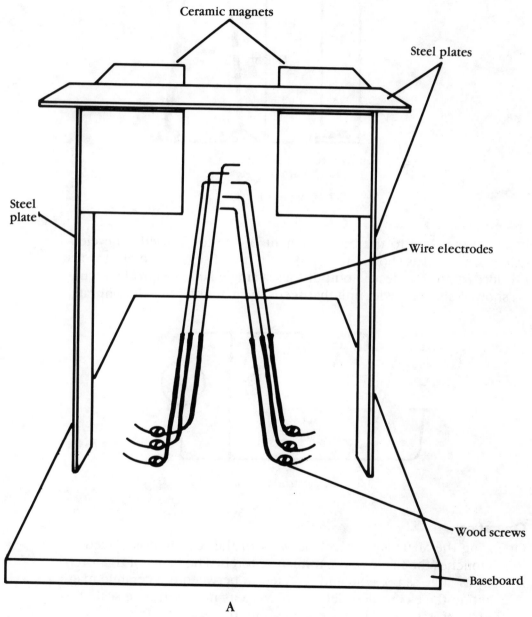

Ceramic magnets

Steel plates

Steel plate

Wire electrodes

Wood screws

Baseboard

A

8-2 The MHD generator.

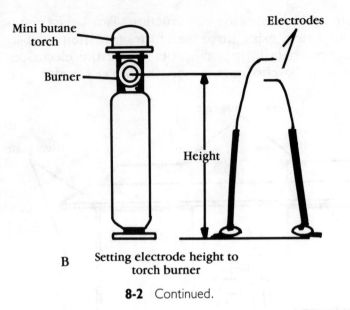

B **Setting electrode height to torch burner**

8-2 Continued.

height is matched to the burner height of the torch used. The electrodes are wired as shown in FIG. 8-3. The use of segmented electrodes produces a greater electric output than a single large electrode. Figure 8-4 shows a simple seeder unit that seeds the gas with potassium nitrate.

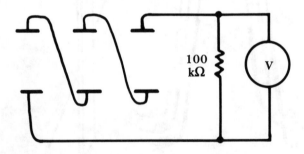

8-3 The electrode wiring.

Operation

Operating the MHD is simple. The wick of the seed unit is placed so that it touches the flame of the miniature torch. The flame of the torch is made as large as possible and directed in between the ceramic magnets hitting the electrodes. Set the VOM to its most-sensitive scale for volts. The prototype MHD produced about 0.1 V.

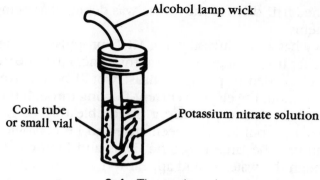

8-4 The seeder unit.

Improving the MHD generator

The model MHD generator is working with a mediocre-temperature gas. A hotter and larger flame from an oxypropane or any number of other torches will improve conductivity of the gas and thus the performance. If you are familiar with the operation of these torches, you might want to give it a try. If not, I advise against experimenting with high-temperature torches.

The ceramic magnets produce about 4000 gauss, which is pretty weak by MHD standards. Replacing the ceramic magnets with stronger electromagnets will increase the electrical power output.

Finally, the electrodes should be replaced with a tungsten or nichromium wire. The standard wire used in the prototype wears out pretty fast. The high-temperature wires will last substantially longer. You might be able to use the tungsten wire filament from burned-out incandescent lamps.

By making these changes, the MHD power produced will become more pronounced. In the prototype, thermo-ionic (gaseous thermocouple) effects contribute more electrical power than the MHD effect.

Liquid metal MHD

Although the project used a gaseous conductor flowing past a magnetic field to induce voltage, a conductive liquid could also be used to achieve the same effect. A liquid metal, such as mercury, has been used in an MHD configuration to produce power.

MHD PROPULSION

Since the movie *The Hunt For Red October*, created from Tom Clancy's best-selling novel, MHD propulsion systems have captured the public's attention. The MHD drive in the movie was depicted as being invisible to sonar systems.

The Navy has and is investigating MHD propulsion systems. However, they are far from being invisible at this time. First, the tremendous magnetic field needed to produce thrust would be relatively easy to pick up. In addition, the electric current flowing through the sea water would electrolyze it, and produce a noticeable trail of gas bubbles. Although MHD propulsion has been stated to be ecologically safe, I have my doubts. The large magnetic fields and high current density flowing through the water would appear to have a negative impact on sea life. As with the MHD generators, superconductive magnets must be used to make the drives practicable.

How MHD propulsion works

Figure 8-5 shows the basic MHD propulsion system. It is similar to the MHD generator. The main difference is that, instead of drawing electric-

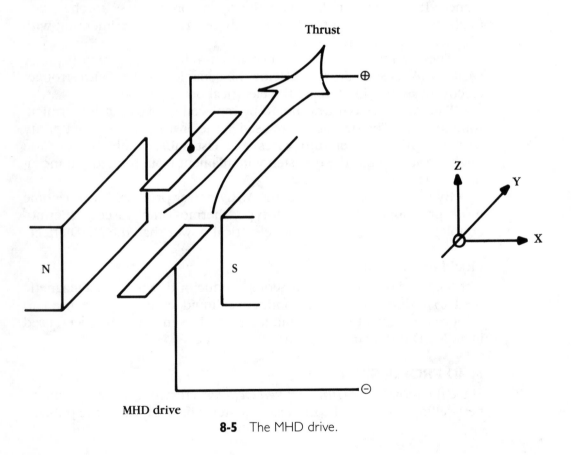

8-5 The MHD drive.

ity via the electrodes, electricity is supplied to flow through between the electrodes. The electrified seawater, being under a strong magnetic field, is propelled perpendicular to the magnetic and electric fields.

MHD propulsion in space MHD propulsion systems seem to be ideally suited for interplanetary space travel. MHD rockets could not replace chemical rockets for the raw power needed to escape Earth's gravitational field because of the MHD's low specific thrust. However, once lifted in space, the MHD propulsion can easily surpass and speed past chemical rockets in traveling to other planets.

The reasons are that, despite their low thrust, the MHDs use very little fuel, and the exhaust velocity of the propellant is very high. Combine these two properties and you have a rocket engine that can run continuously for long periods of time and will allow the vessel to slowly gather to high speed. Remember Newton's law of motion: every action has an opposite and equal reaction. With chemical rockets, regardless of how powerful the thrust is, the rocket can go no faster than the exhaust velocity of its propellant.

The MHD space drive looks like the illustration in FIG. 8-5. The difference is that an ionized gas is released in the MHD chamber. The ionized gas is accelerated as a result of the electric and magnetic fields and produces thrust, in the same manner as described for the sea-water MHD propulsion system.

Parts list:

- Miniature butane torch, Radio Shack
- Large bar magnet, 1 inch × 1 inch × 2 inches, Images Co.
- Steel plate, 1 inch × 4.5 inch × 1/16 inch thick, Images Co.
- Potassium nitrate, 1/2 oz., Images Co.
- Wick, Images Co.

IMAGES COMPANY
P.O. Box 140742
Staten Island, NY 10314
(718) 698-8305

Chapter 9

Plasma acoustics

About 20 years ago, I read an interesting article on three researchers (W. Babcock, K. L. Baker, and A. G. Cattaneo) who discovered an interesting phenomenon of plasma acoustics while working at the United Technology Center in California.

The researchers were able to use a high-temperature plasma as a speaker. They noted that the frequency response of the plasma speaker is much better at high frequencies than at low frequencies. This drawback, however, might be as a result of the small size of the plasma, rather than being an intrinsic limitation. Rather than try to create a high-temperature plasma, you can use a lower temperature flame from a propane or butane torch that is seeded with potassium nitrate.

BASIC OPERATION

Any sound source can be used, but I'd advise using music because it has more high-frequency components in it than speech. The audio source (radio, tape, or CD player) must supply 10 or more watts of power to be heard. If necessary, feed the audio signal through a power amplifier. The more power, the greater the volume. From the amplifier, the audio is fed to a step-up transformer (see FIG. 9-1). The output of the step-up transformer is fed into two electrodes positioned in the flame. The flame is seeded with a water solution of potassium nitrate to induce low-temperature ionization.

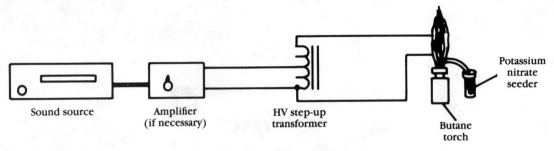

9-1 A diagram of the flame speaker components.

How it works

The torch flame ionizes the potassium nitrate easily, by thermal ionization. Ionization of the potassium in the flame creates free electrons and positive potassium ions. When you supply a high-voltage electrical signal, the positive ions move toward the negative electrode, and the free electrons move toward the positive electrode. This movement, as in the case of an audio signal, switches back and forth rapidly, and causes the flame to vibrate.

Flames, like a liquid, exhibit a surface tension. A gaseous membrane is created by the difference in density and high temperature of the torch flame to the ambient air. This membrane acts as a diaphragm to compress and rarefy the air, and produce sound waves as the flame vibrates.

EXPERIMENTING WITH PLASMA ACOUSTICS

Figure 9-2 illustrates a simple set-up for you to begin experimenting. The seeder I used was fashioned from an old coin tube holder, but any small container will also work. An alcohol lamp wick is used to continuously supply the potassium nitrate into the flame. The potassium nitrate solution strength isn't critical, dump a spoonful in a small quantity of water and it will work fine.

The step-up transformer is a high-voltage auto transformer from Images Co. Be careful when operating the circuit; the audio signal from the amplifier is stepped-up by the transformer and is capable of shocking you.

When running the plasma speaker, if the electrodes start arcing, either move the electrodes further apart or turn down the volume on the amplifier. Remember to turn off all the equipment before adjusting or touching the electrodes. They are connected to the high-voltage transformer and are quite capable of shocking you.

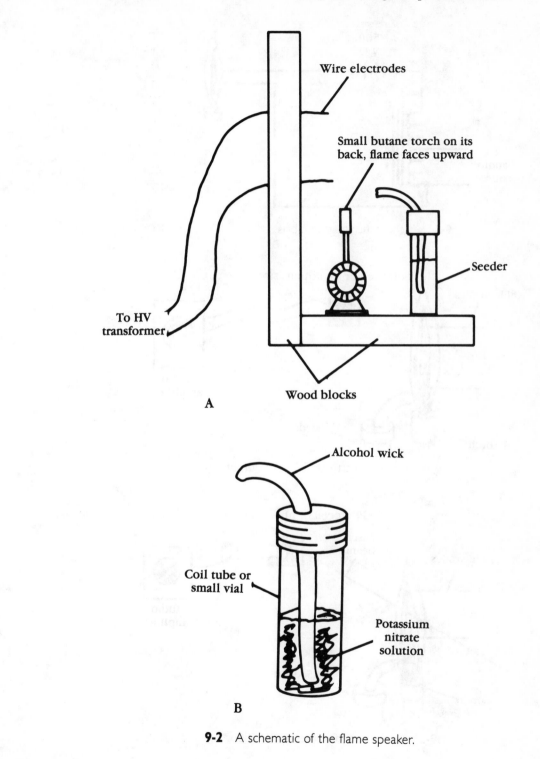

9-2 A schematic of the flame speaker.

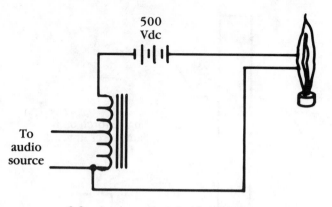

9-3 A schematic to add dc bias.

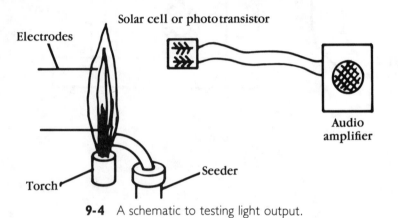

9-4 A schematic to testing light output.

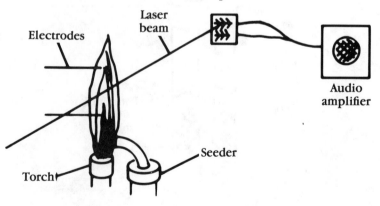

9-5 A schematic for laser modulation.

Improving the design

The experiment can be improved by using a larger and hotter flame. Anything that would do so will increase the quality of the sound. If possible, use nichrome or tungsten wire for the electrodes. These wires will last longer in the high-temperature flame. Finally, supplying a 500 dc bias to the circuit will improve the quality of sound (see FIG. 9-3).

Other experiments

A solar cell or phototransistor that is connected to an audio amplifier will output the sound signal fed into the flame when the light from the flame is directed onto the photocell by a lens (see FIG. 9-4). Another possibility is to direct a laser beam between the electrodes in the flame. This might be a low-cost way to modulate a laser with information (see FIG. 9-5). In the 1920s, Lee DeForest replaced a radio crystal detector with a flame (see FIG. 9-6).

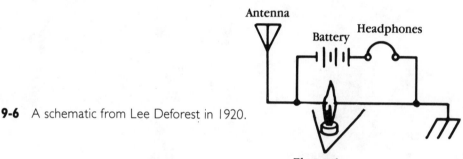

9-6 A schematic from Lee Deforest in 1920.

Lee Deforest 1920
Flame replaced crystal detector

Parts list:

- Miniature butane torch, Radio Shack
- IMT1, HV transformer, Images Co.
- Potassium Nitrate, $1/2$ oz., Images Co.
- Wick, Images Co.

IMAGES COMPANY
P.O. Box 140742
Staten Island, NY 10314
(718) 698-8305

Chapter 10

Expansion cloud chamber

*C*loud chambers are simple devices that allow you to see trails made from atomic particles. The particular chamber we are building is a derivative of a unit described in the April 1956 issue of *Scientific American*. The unit is updated to take advantage of newer materials. I like this cloud chamber for its simplicity and usefulness.

CONSTRUCTION

Figure 10-1 shows the basic construction. It uses two medium-sized clear plastic jars. A large hole is cut into each screw-on lid. The plastic lids are fastened together using epoxy. Use a good amount of epoxy to hold these lids together or the unit will leak (see FIG. 10-2).

A hole is made in the side near the bottom of jars J1 and J2. The hole in J2 is fitted with a plastic elbow, and is secured with a water-resistant cement or epoxy. On the inner end of the tube, a small rubber balloon is attached. Coat the threads on the jar lids with a liberal amount of an aquarium sealant before screwing them on the jars. Allow the sealant to cure.

Fill the jars using a funnel with a plastic tube through the hole on J1. The solution is a 1:1 mixture of alcohol and water. Add to this solution some salt and enough black india ink to turn the solution a dark black.

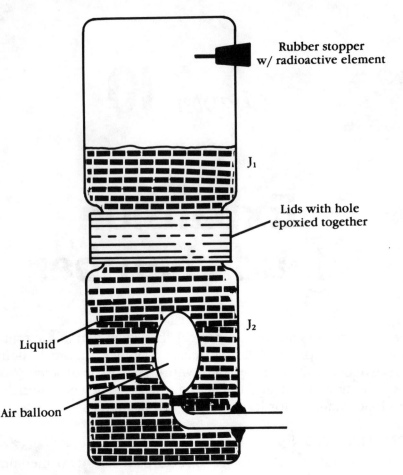

Rubber stopper
w/ radioactive element

J_1

Lids with hole
epoxied together

J_2

Liquid

Air balloon

10-1 A schematic of the cloud chamber.

Radioactive source

Two companies supply radioactive sources that are made especially for
use in a cloud chamber. They are Carolina Biological Supply and the
Nucleus Company. Follow all safety precautions that these companies
recommend when purchasing the material.

Finish off the chamber by gluing or securing a radioactive source
to a rubber stopper. Insert the stopper into the hole in J1. The stopper
should form an airtight fit with the jar. If not, the air will escape when it
is used, rather than compress it, and render the cloud chamber useless.

Use

Using the cloud chamber is straightforward. Inflate the balloon to raise
the liquid an inch or so with a small aquarium-type air pump, or use

10-2 The cloud chamber.

your lungs, if you're healthy enough. Keep the balloon inflated a minute for the compressed air in J1 to reach room temperature. The air is then released, the cooling effect produces clouds in the chamber, which allows the tracks of atomic particles to be seen.

You will be surprised by the force that is required to inflate the balloon. Consequently, the force generated tries to pry the jars apart. Be sure you use enough of a good epoxy to form a good solid seal between the lids or they will leak.

Suppliers for radioactive materials

CAROLINA BIOLOGICAL SUPPLY
2700 York Road
Burlington, NC 27215
(919) 584-0381

THE NUCLEUS CO.
761 Emory Valley Road
Oak Ridge, TN 37830-2561
(615) 482-4041

Chapter **11**

Nitinol-shaped memory alloy

Shaped memory alloys (SMA) have some interesting properties. One property of the material is that it contracts when it is heated. This property is similar to the contraction of muscle tissue. Notice that this effect is the opposite of standard metals, which expand when heated and contract when cooled. Using this material, you can achieve electrical movement without using motors, stepper motors, or solenoids.

Another property of the material is called the *Shaped Memory Effect (SME)*. Simply put, this material will, when heated to a critical temperature, return to a predefined shape that it has been trained to remember. So, an object made of this metal material could be twisted, bent, and folded out of shape, then heated to return the object to its original shape. It's fascinating to watch this happen; as the material is heated, it quickly unbends, unfolds, and untwists itself back into its original shape—kind of like self healing.

HISTORY

In 1932, Arne Olander, a Swedish researcher, discovered the Shaped Memory Effect in a gold-cadmium (Au-Cd) alloy. In 1951, two researchers, L. C. Chang and T. H. Read analyzed the crystal structure and changes of the Shaped Memory Effect in the Au-Cd alloy. In 1958, these two researchers made a cyclic weight-lifting device to be displayed at the Brussels World Fair.

In 1961, William Beuhler, who worked at U.S. Naval Labs, discovered SME in an alloy of titanium-nickel. At the time, the Beuhler team was looking to develop a heat- and corrosion-resistant alloy. In any case, this alloy was by far cheaper and safer to work with than any SME alloy to date. The team named the new alloy *nitinol* (pronounced "night-in-all"). The material's name is representative of its elemental components and place of origin. The "Ni" and "Ti" are the atomic symbols for nickel and titanium, the "nol" represents the Naval Ordnance Laboratory, where it was discovered.

In the 1960s and 1970s, other alloys were discovered that exhibited SME. In 1985, Dr. Dai Homma of Japan's Toki Corporation announced an improved version of nitinol. This improved version of nitinol is sold in this country under the tradename BioMetal. Mondo-Tronics in California sells nitinol wire under the tradename of Flexinol (see suppliers). References to either Flexinol, BioMetal, Muscle Wire, or nitinol are to be considered one and the same.

APPLICATIONS

Many interesting applications of this material has been put forth. NASA had proposed using nitinol to make spacecraft antennas, which would deploy when heated by the sun, or a secondary heating unit.[1] More down to earth ventures are its use in eye-glass frames, dental alignment material, pumps, blood filters, solenoids, and artificial hearts.

HOW IT WORKS

The properties of nitinol rely upon the crystal structure of the material. The structure is sensitive to both external stress and temperature. Before the actual mechanics involved can be covered, the temperature phases of the material must first be defined.

Parent phase Material above transition temperature. Transition temperature depends on the exact composition of material. For the nitinol wire, you are working with a temperature of 100 to 130 °C (190 to 260 °F). This temperature is where the wire contracts or returns to a previously defined shape. The crystal structure is cubic.

Martensitic phase Material below transition temperature. The crystal structure is needlelike and is collected in small domains. Within each domain, the crystals are aligned. The material is cool and can be bent or formed into other shapes. This external stress transforms the

---

[1] *55-nitinol,* C.M. Jackson. NASA Pub. SP-5110, Washington, DC, 1972.

crystal structure of the material. It is sometimes called *stress-induced martensite*.

Annealing phase At this temperature, the material will reorient its crystal structure to remember its present shape. The annealing phase for the material you are working with is 540°C.

When a cooled wire is bent or twisted, the crystal structure is transformed. If the wire is now heated above its transition temperature (parent phase), the crystal structure changes from needlelike to cubic. Because the cubic crystals don't fit into the same space as the needle-like crystals, they are formed under strain. To relieve this strain, they move and change their positions. This "least strain" position is the original shape (the annealed shape) of the material. Where the wire hasn't any stress-induced transformations, the crystal structure still changes, but results in no net movement. [2] [3]

PROPERTIES

Nitinol metal can generate a shape-resuming force of about 22,000 pounds per square inch. You will not be working with a square inch of material; it will be a 6-mil wire. Even so, a 6-mil wire (0.006 inch diameter) can generate a contractive force of 11 ounces. If you want more pull, simply multiply the wires until you reach the required contractive force. The wire can contract up to 10% of its length. For longer lifetime (greater than 1,000,000 cycles) restrict the contraction to only 6% of its length.

The easiest way to heat the wire is by passing an electric current through it. Take care not to overheat the wire or its properties will degrade. The wire has an electrical resistance of a little less than one ohm per inch. The Flexinol is supplied with crimp terminals (see FIG. 11-1). These terminals are used to connect to the material because the Flexinol wire should not be raised to the high temperature that would be required for soldering.

The reaction time can be quite short, measured in milliseconds. In addition, full strength is developed at the beginning of the cycle. This property is in contrast to standard solenoids, which develop full strength near the end of their cycle. The nitinol material is stronger

---

[2] "On the Thermodynamics of Thermoelastic Martensitic Transformations." R.J. Salzbrenner and Moris Cohen, *Acta Metallurgica*. Vol 27, No. 5, May 1979.
[3] "Shaped-Memory Alloys." L. McDonald Schetky, *Scientific American*, Vol. 241, 11/79.

Crimp terminal, supplied w/ Flexinol wire

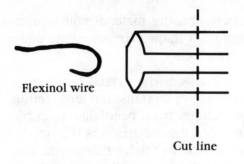

Flexinol wire

Cut line

II-I Making crimp terminal connections.

Procedure:
1. Insert Flexinol wire in channel
2. Grip channel w/pliers
3. Cut off excess channel

To solder wire:
1. Solder power wire to channel
2. Go to procedure

than many steels. The 6-mil wire has a breaking strength of about 6 pounds.

Wire diameter

Nitinol wire, as stated previously, is sold under the trade name of Flexinol from Mondo-Tronics. The wire diameter is given in micrometers as a number suffix of the name Flexinol. So, Flexinol 150 is a nitinol wire with a diameter of 150 micrometers. To convert micrometers to inches, multiple by 0.00003937. Doing the multiplication, you find that the diameter of Flexinol 150 is 6 mils (0.006 inch).

ACTIVATING NITINOL WIRE

As stated, the nitinol wire is activated by passing an electric current through the wire. The wire's resistance to the current heats the wire and causes it to contract. The volume of the wire doesn't change during contraction. So, as the wire decreases in length, its diameter increases by a proportional amount, keeping the volume the same. The activation temperature of the wire is 100 to 130°C (190 to 260°F).

Direct electric heating

Nitinol wire can be activated with *direct electric heating* using a low voltage, such as that from a 9-V transistor battery. A simple circuit can be constructed using a battery, a switch, and a small length of nitinol (see FIG. 11-2). Take care not to overheat the wire. In addition, direct electric heating doesn't heat the wire evenly. Connections to the nitinol will draw heat away from the ends of the wire. This results in the center of the wire heating faster than the ends. So, although direct electric heating works, a better method is pulse-width modulation.

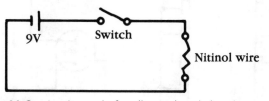

11-2   A schematic for direct electric heating.

Pulse-width modulation heating

Heating the wire is more efficiently controlled with *pulse-width modulation (PWM) heating*. Here, a square wave from a simple circuit is used to turn on and off the electric current. Depending on the frequency and duty cycle of the square wave, you can adjust the amount of contraction and maintain the wire in contracted condition for a longer period of time. Because of the rapid on and off, the wire has time to distribute the heat and results in a more uniform heating. This method is used in this book.

CIRCUIT

Usually a 555 timer is used to provide a square wave to activate nitinol wire. Although this is a good stand-alone method it wouldn't allow for easy interfacing to a computer. This circuit is designed around a 4011 quad NAND gate (see FIG. 11-3). The NAND gate is made to generate a square wave, much like a 555 timer, which can be operated as a stand-alone circuit using a switch, or interfaced to any computer by connecting the circuit to a port line that can be brought high and low under program control. The output of the 4011 is connected to an npn transistor, which is capable of switching a higher current than is required of the nitinol wire. The circuit can be wired on a prototype breadboard using a manual switch to activate the nitinol.

Nitinol demonstration

To demonstrate the potential of this material, you need to build a small mechanical device. If you're like me, you'll want to build the simplest

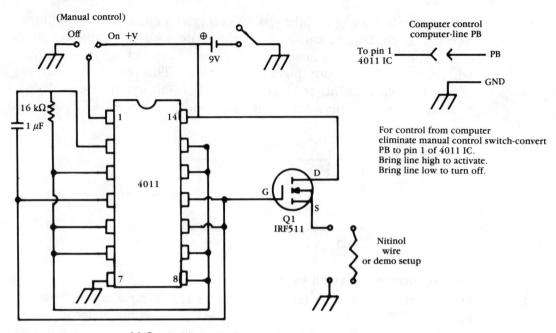

11-3 A schematic for a pulse-width modulation circuit.

unit to start with. To make our electric muscle, the materials you'll need are three machine screws with six nuts, a piece of perfboard or plastic, a small rubber band, and (of course) a length of Flexinol (nitinol) material.

The machine screws, nuts, and perfboard are available from Radio Shack (see the parts list). The nitinol wire is available from Mondo-Tonics under its trade name of Flexinol (see the suppliers). You have to find the rubber band yourself.

Look at FIG. 11-4. Drill three holes in the perfboard to accommodate the machine screws in a triangle pattern, as shown. The Flexinol wire is connected to the two top screws. The rubber band is looped around the bottom machine screw, and the nitinol wire is looped through the top of the rubber band. To determine the distance, place the bottom machine screw and stretch the rubber band from a position that is parallel with the top screws and down. Remember, the nitinol has a pull of about 11 ounces, so don't make the rubber band so tight that the nitinol isn't able to contract and move upwards. However, it should be tight enough for it to take up the slack of the nitinol wire when it is relaxed.

For the connections from the circuit to the nitinol, I used small

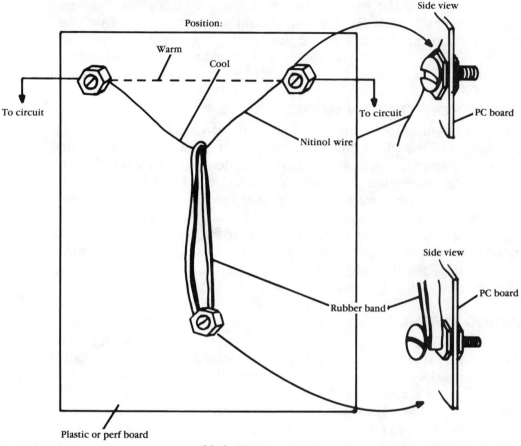

11-4 The test fixture.

jumper cables connected to the back of the machine screws to the circuit. You could, of course, simply use wire.

When the unit is activated, the wire gets hot, contracts, and pulls up from the rubber band. When the unit is deactivated, the wire cools, elongates, and lowers into its resting position.

Use

When you have the circuit wired and the demo electric muscle unit built, apply power to the circuit. The control switch allows you to contract the muscle by putting the switch in the +Voltage setting. Connecting the switch to ground will turn off the square-wave generator and the electric muscle will relax. My unit performed slowly, probably as a result of the high tension that I had on it. I also had no hesitation about overdriving the wire; I'm not concerned with making the wire last for one million cycles. You still should be careful not to overheat the wire. You can check if you're overheating the circuit by touching the transistor. If it is hot, you can assume that the wire is overheating. To reduce the current, add another 10-Ω resistor in line with the first.

2ND DEMONSTRATION MODEL

The second nitinol actuator shows how you can amplify the mechanical motion of the wire using a lever (see FIG. 11-5). The lever pivots on screw A. The nitinol wire is attached to the lever and to screw E. The wire is threaded around the other screws (B,C, and D). When activated, the lever rises. The lever can be made from any material: wood, plastic, or metal. If you use a metal lever, you can make the electrical connection to the wire through screws A and E. If the lever is made from a nonconductive material, use screws B and E for the electrical connections. If the lever is too light, you might need to add some weight on the end of it so that it lowers easily when the nitinol is deactivated.

GOING FURTHER

This chapter has just scratched the surface of the applications that can be derived using this material. It is quite possible to build a realistic android hand. As an example, a simple digit flexer is illustrated in FIG. 11-6. This unit is constructed of three-hole soft rubber stopper or silicone tubing. The nitinol wire is threaded in a loop through the two outer holes. A copper wire is threaded up through the center hole. The loop of nitinol wire and the end of the copper wire is crimped in a small terminal (see FIG. 11-1). By applying current between the copper wire and one end of the nitinol, you can make the tube flex right (A-C) or left (B-C). By applying power to the two ends of the nitinol wire, the tube will flex backwards.

Heat engines are another fertile field for experimentation and development. One company sells a toy boat that is powered by nitinol wire. The boat has a small cargo bay for ice. The temperature difference between the ice and the water that the boat rests in powers the toy boat.

You might want to attempt to "train" a piece of nitinol wire to a particular shape. You can do this by bending the wire to the shape you want, clamping it in position and heating it to about 540 °C. You also might want to try direct electric heating it to reach the annealing temperature.

Mondo-Tronics sells a book titled "Working with Shaped Memory

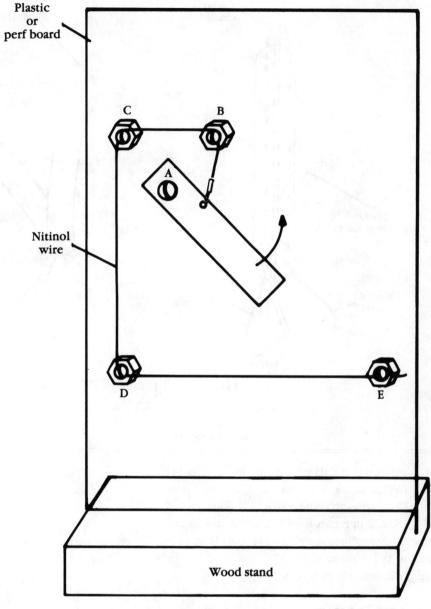

Plastic
or
perf board

Nitinol
wire

C   B

A

D   E

Wood stand

II-5 The lever.

Wires,'' which shows various actuators and uses of this material. Several samples of nitinol wires with various diameters are included with the book. It is a worthwhile investment if you plan on doing any experimenting with nitinol.

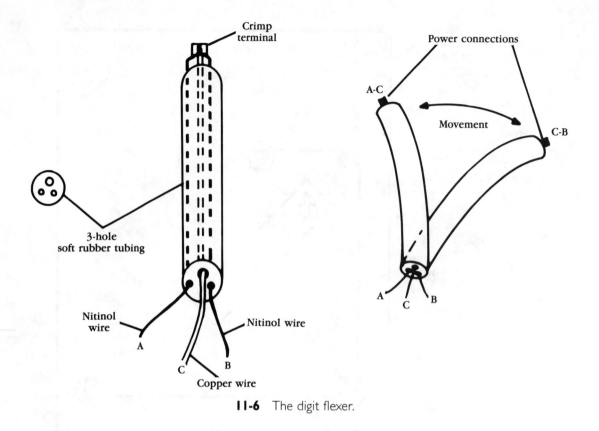

11-6   The digit flexer.

PWM parts list

IC1   4011 quad NAND gate, Radio Shack, 276-2411
C1   1-μF capacitor, Radio Shack, 272-1434
R1   15-kΩ resistor, Radio Shack, 271-036
Q1   2N2222 npn transistor, Radio Shack, 276-1617
Shape Memory Wire Guidebook, Mondo-Tronics, 3-074
Flexinol, 150 × 40 inches, 3-072
Misc. switches, 9-V battery, and cap.

Demo 1 and 2 parts list

Round-head machine screws, 6-32 × 3/4 inch, Radio Shack, 64-3012
Hex nuts, 6-32, Radio Shack, 64-3019
Perf board (or plastic), Radio Shack, 276-147

Available from :

MONDO-TRONICS
2476 Verna Court
San Leandro, CA 94577
(501) 351-5930
(800) 374-5764

Chapter **12**

Air-pollution monitor

*I*n this project, you will build an air-pollution monitor that can sniff and detect various airborne compounds. The heart of the circuit is a TGS gas sensor. The circuit can easily be interfaced to a computer and allows the computer to sense its environment for a number of toxic compounds. The most obvious use for the simple circuit is as an automatic ventilation control.

SEMICONDUCTOR SENSOR

The sensor material is N-type sintered SnO_2 (tin dioxide). When a combustible or reducing gas is absorbed on the sensor's surface, the resistance of the sensor decreases dramatically. This makes it an easy job to build a detection circuit or computer interface.

The SnO_2 must be heated to a high temperature for it to become useful as a gas sensor. The sensor contains a small internal heating coil that heats the SnO_2 material inside the sensor to between 200 and 400°C. Many other sensor materials perform just as well as SnO_2, but the SnO_2 is the preferred material of use because of its chemical stability.

Gases detected by the sensor

Inorganic gases   Ammonia, carbon monoxide, hydrogen, and hydrogen cyanide.

Hydrocarbons and derivatives   Methane, ethane, propane, butane, pentane, hexane, heptane, octane, decane, petroleum ether, petroleum benzine, gasoline, kerosene, petroleum naphtha, acetylene, ethylene, propylene, butadiene, butylene, benzene, toluene, o-xylene, m-xylene, and ethylene oxide.

Alcohols   Methanol, ethanol, n-propanol, iso-propanol, n-butanol, and iso-butanol.

Ethers   Methyl ether and ethyl ether.

Ketones   Acetone and methyl ethyl ketone.

Esters   Methyl acetate, ethyl acetate, n-propyl acetate, iso-propyl acetate, n-butyl acetate, and iso-butyl acetate.

Nitrogen compounds   Nitro methane, mono methyl amine, dimethyl-amine, trimethyl amine, mono ethyl amine, and diethyl amine.

Halogenized hydrocarbons   Methyl chloride, methylene chloride, ethyl chloride, ethylene chloride, ethylidene chloride, trichloroethane, vinylidene chloride, trichloro ethylene, methyl bromide, and vinyl chloride.

Although the sensor is capable of detecting these compounds, it cannot tell us which of the many gases it is detecting. Ongoing research and development is working on constructing sensors that can determine particular compounds.

FUTURE SENSORS

Humans do not have an acute sense of smell when compared to other mammals, such as dogs. Even so, each of us has about 2 million olfactory sensors in our nasal cavities that can detect thousands of different smells.

It's interesting to note that the nose and nasal passages originally had nothing to do with respiration, but began separately as a smelling device. Smelling is a primitive function, and our smelling apparatus developed into respiratory passages.

For instance, fish have nostrils, but they do not breath through them. To breath, fish take water in through their mouth. The nostrils are used for smelling (sensing) and locating food.

It might be some time before artificial sensors meet the diversity and sensitivity of even the human olfactory. But what artificial sensors lack in diversity they might more than make up for in sensitivity. One scheme under development uses 12 SnO_2 sensors simultaneously. Each of the sensors is made slightly different from the others. Naturally, each sensor reacts a little differently when detecting a particular compound. This information is gathered simultaneously from the 12 sensors and is stored as a gas profile in a computer's memory bank. When an unknown gas is presented for analysis, not only is the gas detected, but the type of gas is determined by matching its unique profile from the profiles stored in the computer's memory.

The uses for these more sophisticated sensors are varied. They can be used in food-processing equipment to check for food spoilage. The fragrance industry can use them to mix and match fragrances or to make inexpensive perfumes that more closely match expensive perfumes. Biologists might use them to detect and measure human pheromones or hormonal changes in humans and other mammals.

Sensor characteristics

Figure 12-1 is a cut-away illustration of the sensor. The sensor has the appearance of a short 6-pin orange plastic tube. The top and bottom of the sensor is covered with 100-mesh stainless steel wire cloth. The heart of the sensor is the cylindrical form in the middle of the unit. The cylinder is a ceramic material with the SnO_2 material deposited on its surface. The heater coil is located inside the ceramic cylinder. The heater has a resistance of 38 Ω.

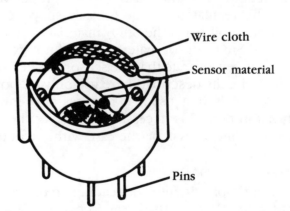

Wire cloth

Sensor material

Pins

12-1 A cut-away view of the gas sensor.

Figure 12-2 shows the pinout schematic of the sensor. Pins 1 and 3 are internally connected, as are pins 4 and 6. Pins 2 and 5 connect to the heater coil. The heater is not polarized, so the +5-V supply voltage for the heater can be connected to either pin. Figure 12-3 shows the bottom of the sensor and pin location.

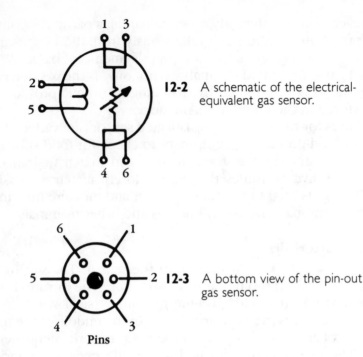

12-2 A schematic of the electrical-equivalent gas sensor.

12-3 A bottom view of the pin-out gas sensor.

Pins

The heater requires a regulated +5 V for proper operation and draws 130 mA. This regulated voltage is easily supplied using a 7805 regulator. The heater coil heats the SnO_2 material. The circuit voltage passing through the SnO_2 sensor material should not exceed 24 V. The specifications on the sensor state that the sensor can be used with an ac or dc voltage. The circuits described here use only dc power.

When the sensor is first used, it requires a 15-minute break-in period. The break-in period is necessary whenever the sensor hasn't been used for some time, as will be the case with the one you receive.

TEST CIRCUIT

Figure 12-4 shows a simple circuit. The reading on the voltmeter in this set-up is about 0.5 to 1 V (after the break-in period). When the sensor detects any compound, its resistance drops and causes the reading on the voltmeter to jump up to 5 V or more. The actual meter reading depends on the concentration of the gas.

Use the circuit to test the response of various compounds that you have around your home, such as: glue, rubber cement, bleach, alcohol, cleaning fluid, etc. It's enough to bring the material close to the sensor for a reaction; do not spray anything on the sensor.

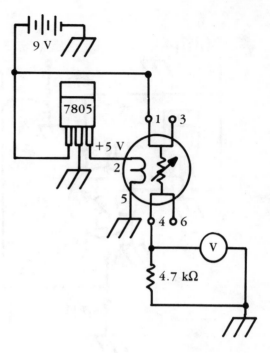

12-4 A schematic of the test circuit.

Simple air-pollution monitor

Figure 12-5 is a simple go/no-go air-pollution monitor. The circuit uses two comparators of a standard 339 quad comparator IC. The green LED is lit as long as the gas sensor doesn't detect any airborne compounds. When the circuit does detect a gas, the green LED turns off and the red LED turns on.

Nothing is critical about the circuit, point-to-point wiring is fine. Although you can solder wires directly to the TGS gas sensor pins, it might be a better idea to purchase a socket along with the sensor. The socket makes it easy to mount the sensor on the outside of the small instrument case.

When the circuit is completed, it must be calibrated. This is a simple procedure. Turn on the circuit and allow a warm-up period. If this is the first time for the sensor to be used, wait 15 minutes before you calibrate the circuit. If not, two to five minutes will suffice. To calibrate, adjust potentiometer R2 to the point where the green LED is about to go off and the red LED is about to turn on. That's it; it's calibrated.

To test the circuit, bring the sensor close to your mouth and breathe on it. The green LED should go out and the red LED should turn on. The sensor is detecting the carbon monoxide from your breath. The LEDs should go back to their normal mode in 15 to 30 sec-

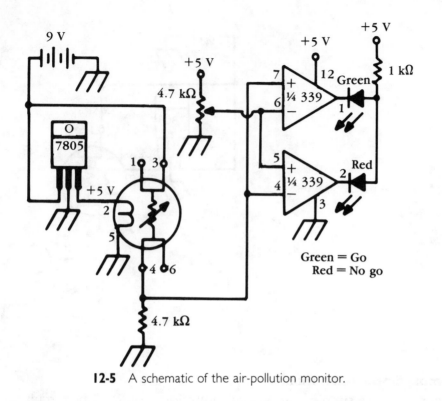

12-5 A schematic of the air-pollution monitor.

onds, depending on the air circulation. You also might want to release some gas from a butane lighter (unlit), or open a bottle of alcohol by the sensor as a test.

Because the heater section of the sensor draws 130 mA, I advise using an 9-V alkaline battery for portable operation. However, any battery you use will wear out pretty fast. The best power supply is a plug-in transformer to supply 9 Vdc to the circuit.

GOING FURTHER

The sensor can be used as a:

- Gas-leak detector
- Carbon-monoxide detector
- Automatic ventilation controller
- Fire alarm (detects combustible gases in smoke)
- Alcohol detector
- Air-pollution monitor

This sensor can easily be interfaced to a computer. The comparator is set to trip when the resistance of the sensor drops (this is the equivalent of the red LED section in the simple air-pollution monitor). The comparator will output a +5-V signal, which can be read off of the computer's interface line; when the sensor detects a gas, the +5-V line will drop to ground.

By connecting an analog-to-digital converter in place of the comparator, the computer can read the changes in resistance and thus it can also read the concentrations of the gas it is detecting. Sensitivity can be improved by placing the sensor in the arm of a balanced resistance bridge. The output of the bridge is then connected to a standard op amp for amplification. When the sensor detects a minute amount of gas, the bridge is thrown out of balance, and the resulting signal is amplified by the op amp.

Parts list

R1	4.7-kΩ resistor, Radio Shack, 271-1330
R2	4.7-kΩ potentiometer, Radio Shack, 271-281
R3	1-kΩ resistor, Radio Shack, 271-1321
IC1	7805 voltage regulator, Radio Shack, 276-1770
IC2	339 comparator, Radio Shack, 276-1712
D1	Green LED, Radio Shack, 276-022
D2	Red LED, Radio Shack, 276-041
H1	Snap-in holders for LEDs, Radio Shack, 276-079
Misc.	Instrument case, 9-V battery and cap., switch, PC board.
822	TGS gas sensor and data sheet, Allegro Electronic Systems
822A	Socket for TGS sensor, Allegro Electronic Systems

ALLEGRO ELECTRONIC SYSTEMS
3 Mine Mountain Road
Cornwall Bridge, CT 06754
(203) 672-0123

Chapter **13**

Neural networks

Neural networks are computer operating systems that attempt to function and learn based on the biological system of the brain. One of the first questions that comes to mind is "why model the brain?" Computers are functioning pretty well without neurons. Well, computers are quite limited when asked to do some simple things in real time, such as identify speech or a picture. The ability of neural networks to accomplish these (and other) tasks in real time is best described by an analogy.

Suppose your friend is standing about twenty feet away from you. He looks at you and yells "catch!" as he throws a baseball toward you. You see the ball coming, move to the right, raise your arm, the ball hits your hand, and you catch it.

Although this is a simple task for humans, it is extremely difficult to program the actions in a computer. The factors needed to be programed are:

1. Hearing the command and understanding it; to catch is much different than to duck.

2. Visually lock onto the ball.

3. Track the ball and estimate the initial velocity of the ball.

4. Calculate the trajectory through three-dimensional space, then moving a catching unit, from a rest point in three-dimensional space to another point in three-dimensional space, where the ball was hit.

5. Catch the ball in real time. If you ask a computer to do all of this, the ball would be rolling 20 feet behind it as it was calculating the initial velocity and trajectory of the ball.

Neural nets, on the other hand, do not perform calculations. In this way, they act like a biological system. If it was your job to catch the ball, you would not be standing there performing calculus equations to see where the ball would end up. You would instinctively, without any math whatsoever, estimate where the ball is going and catch it. How did you accomplish this task without using math? You learned it. Probably by missing hundreds of balls thrown to you, but remembering what you did when you actually caught or came close to catching the ball.

It's the same way with neural nets; they are taught. To teach a neural net to catch a ball, you don't fill it up with equations. You assign it a task "catch the ball," then you keep throwing balls to it. In the beginning, its motions are completely random. But every time it comes close, even by accident, that procedure is reinforced (strengthened) in the neural network, which is called *supervised learning*. Naturally, the more a certain procedure is reinforced, the more likely it will occur. With continual training, the robot will always come close to catching the ball and occasionally hitting the catching mitt. Soon, the ball will always hit the catching mitt. Finally, the neural network will learn how to catch. All without a single equation. Pretty neat, huh?

BIOLOGICAL NEURONS

The brain is a pretty sophisticated piece of wet ware. It is made of special cells, called *neurons (nerve cells)*. The human brain has about 10^{12} ·(1,000 billion) neurons. Neurons have inputs, called *dendrites* and outputs, called *axons* (see FIG. 13-1). The axons connect to the dendrites of other neurons. There isn't a precise number of inputs or outputs to any neuron. A neuron might have 1,000 inputs and a single output, vice versa, or anything in between. For instance, a brain cell might have so many dendrites coming out of it that it looks like a tree. Motor neurons have long axons that run from the central nervous system to the muscle. Sensory neurons generally have a single fiber.

The connection between the dendrite of one neuron and the axon of another is called a *synapse*. This is where information is transmitted. The transmission speed is slow by computer standards, but the brain has a tremendous advantage over computers, *parallelism*. Computers perform operations *serially*, one after another after another, in the standard Von Neuumann computer architecture. The brain however operates with massive parallel structures.

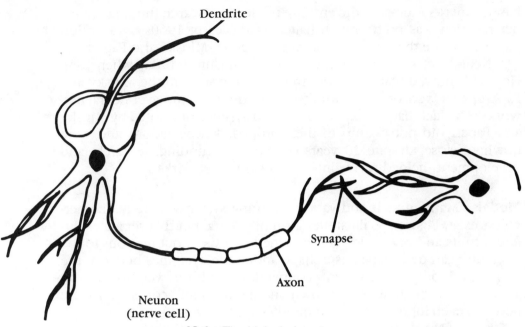

13-1 The biological neuron.

Human brain

The human cerebral cortex has about 100 billion (10^{11})neurons. Each cell has about 1,000 dendrites that make up about 100,000 billion (10^{14}) synapses. If you assume that the brain operates at about 10 Hz, it performs 1,000,000 billion (10^{15}) interconnections per second. Humbly, the brain weighs in at about three lbs.

As you can imagine, to build a neural structure that mimics the brain is beyond our current capabilities. These massive parallel structures allow us to do things that are very hard or impossible for a computer to do. For instance: think; see; identify objects, faces, and colors; hear; remember; act; and create. Simple language processing alone, far exceeds any computer capabilities to date.

In the beginning Neurobiologists who study the brain have made mathematic models of nerve cell behavior. Based on these models, work began in the 1940s and 1950s to build computer devices that model some aspects of the human nervous system. Reasonable success had been achieved by Frank Rosenblatt with his Perceptron work. However, at this time in computer history, there was a division of thought as to what avenue of computer research would lead the way to develop artificial intelligence in computers: neural networks or rule-based expert systems. In the ensuing battle for research funding, neural net research was pretty much halted in the early 1960s by a critical paper from the then current computer experts, Minsky and Papert.

Neural net research didn't resume again until 1982, when John Hopfield showed that the XOR limitations reported in the Minsky and Papert paper were only true for the most primitive two-layer neural networks. The fact that the expert rule-based systems promoted by Minsky and Papert did not live up to their proposed expectations and were nowhere close, despite 20 years of exclusive funding, research, and development, helped revive interest in neural networks.

Models Many models and various learning systems using neural networks exist. Figure 13-2 illustrates a simple neural net that separates different fruits and vegetables. It is assumed that the input neurons to the computer can determine basic shape and color. The lines between the inputs and outputs represent connections, whose weights can be adjusted. Although it isn't shown in the diagram, connections are between each input neuron and middle-layer neuron (fully connected). However, just the strong connections are shown with lines.

To start teaching, the first pattern is introduced to the inputs, for example: red and round. The target answer is apple. The weights or

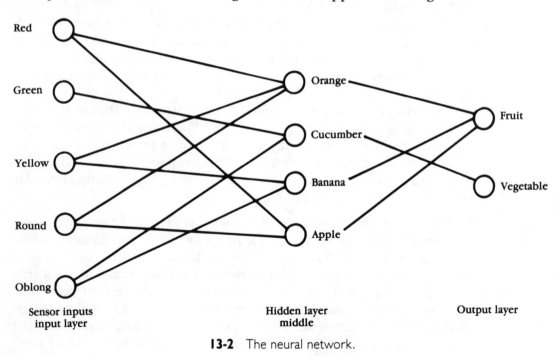

13-2 The neural network.

interconnections between the input/output are modified so that these two properties converge to apple. This is shown by the lines between the red and round inputs to the middle layer, apple. All other connections are made weaker and do not show on the diagram. Similarly, other patterns are introduced and the weights are adjusted to output the correct answer.

Computer modeling   Neural computers are still in their infancy. Manufacturers and chip designers are beginning to introduce neural and fuzzy logic chips. So far, most neural networks are modeled on standard serial computers.

It is important to note that it is doubtful that neural networks will be used exclusively in designing computers and programs. Future computers will use procedures from the rule-based serial; expert system databases, as well as parallel neural networks, will use a collaboration of techniques to perform functions. Whatever technique is most appropriate for the task at hand will be used.

As an example, you would not use a neural network to calculate your tax return. The fuzzy logic would be imprecise. In this case, you would use a standard serial rule-based program. If you were trying to identify a rock using measured properties, such as hardness and density, you might end up using an expert system. Neural networks are more appropriately used for other tasks, such as voice recognition and pattern identification.

Neural networks are superior to serial rule-based programs in some computational tasks and these are being utilized today: mortgage loan applications, life insurance policies, and stock market analysis.

Electronic neurons   Individual neurons by themselves are not intelligent, but if you wire billions of them together, as in the human brain, intelligence emerges.

The most primitive concept in neural networks is the neuron. The electronic equivalent of a biological neuron is shown in FIG. 13-3. Different types of neurons exist. Neurons can perform summation, difference, or signal inversion of the inputs. How the neuron responds to the input is based on its threshold value. When the threshold value is met or exceeded, it becomes active. Activated neurons can also respond differently; some neurons are *excitory*, they fire when stimulated, and others are *inhibitory*, they don't fire when stimulated. Some neurons are stronger than others. To use the proper terminology, they carry more weight; they are able to stimulate or inhibit more neurons than

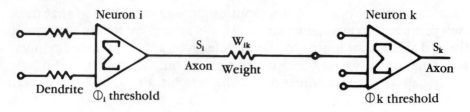

13-3 An electronic neuron.

others. Typically, neurons are not digital in nature, although they can be simulated with digital circuits.

With the upcoming section, you can build a simple electronic neuron and use it as a self-contained control system.

SUN-TRACKER NEURAL CIRCUIT

The circuit in FIG. 13-4 is a basic neural net. The purpose of this net is to steer or look toward a light source, such as the sun.

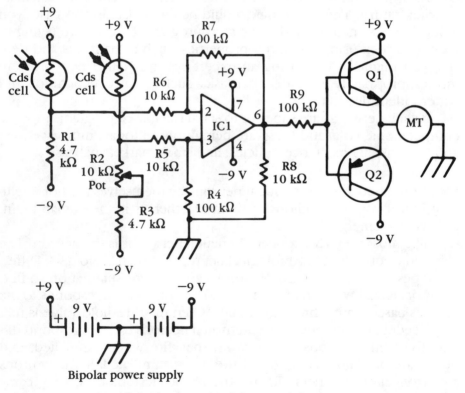

13-4 A schematic of the neural circuit.

The operation of the circuit is simple. Two cadmium sulfide photoresistors act as neural sensors and form neural inputs to your neuron, the 741 op amp. Figure 13-5 illustrates how the input operates. As long as the sun is directly aligned with the two photoresistors, they are equally exposed, and the inputs to the neuron balance out. As the sun moves across the sky, the alignment is thrown off, making one of the inputs stronger than the other. The 741 op-amp neuron activates a small dc motor, moves the tracker up or down, depending on which input is stronger to bring the tracker back into alignment.

The two transistors, Q1 and Q2, read the signal from the 741 op-amp neuron and activate the motor. They might also be considered to be neurons because they only become active when their threshold is reached.

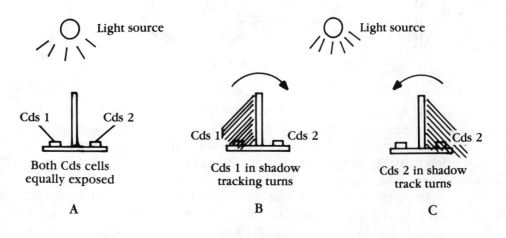

13-5 A detail of the neural input (A, B, and C) and the prototype (D).

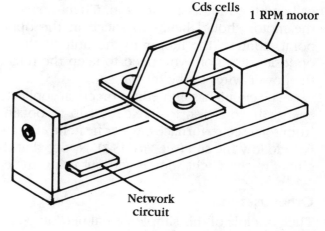

The motor used in the prototype is a 1-rpm 12-Vdc motor. Just about any low-voltage dc motor can be used. Radio Shack sells inexpensive hobby motors, but the rpm on these motors is pretty high. If you use one of these motors, you will need to gear it (see FIG. 13-6).

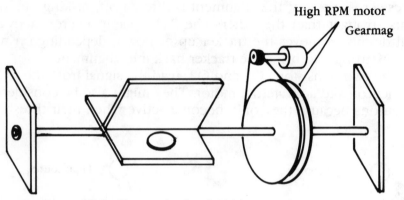

13-6 The gearing for the high-rpm motor.

If this circuit is used with an artificial light source, no modifications are necessary. If you use it to track the sun, you might have to cover the photocells with a piece of colored plastic to cut down on the light intensity. The sun is such a strong light source that it will easily saturate the photocells.

To train the circuit, expose both photocells to equal light, and adjust potentiometer R2 until the motor stops. To test the circuit, cover one photocell and the motor should begin rotating. Uncover the photocell and the motor should stop. Then, cover the other photocell and the motor should begin to rotate in the opposite direction. At this point, connect the motor to the unit. If the motor is turning in the opposite direction, you need to keep the tracker aligned; just reverse the power wires to the motor.

The circuit has immediate practical applications in the field of solar energy. If you wish to track the sun to obtain the maximum output from solar: cells, furnaces, water heaters, etc., the sun tracker will faithfully follow the sun (see FIG. 13-7). Notice that this experimental neural circuit tracks a light source without using any equations.

Other uses

The principle of this simple neural net can be applied to other tracking problems. As the network stands, it can move up or down to track a

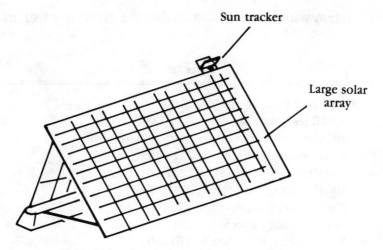

13-7 Using the tracker with a large solar array.

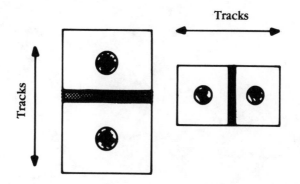

13-8 The configuration for using four neural inputs.

light source. A similar net can be incorporated to operate in the same manner for horizontal directions (see FIG. 13-8). If you changed the four inputs from photocells to radio antennas, it could track radio-emitting satellites across the sky. Because the net is self correcting, once it locked onto the satellite, you would not need to know its orbit.

Obviously, this type of self-correcting tracking system has military potential. Change the inputs to small independent radar systems and you have a ground tracking device for incoming aircraft, missiles, and rockets. The ground tracking could be used for aiming defense systems, such as missiles or lasers.

Place a miniature neural system on a missile connected to its flight control and you have a ground-to-air or air-to-air tracking system. Using the same system with sonar would enable the creation of smart torpedoes.

Parts list

IC1	741 op amp, Radio Shack, 276-007
R1, R3	4.7-kΩ resistor, Radio Shack, 271-1330
R2	10-kΩ potentiometer, Radio Shack, 271-282
R4, R5, R8	10-kΩ resistor, Radio Shack, 271-1335
R6, R7	100-kΩ resistor, Radio Shack, 271-1347
R9	100-Ω resistor, Radio Shack, 271-1311
Cds	Photocells (5/pak), Radio Shack, 276-1657
Q1	Npn transistor, Radio Shack, 276-1617
Q2	Pnp transistor, Radio Shack, 276-1604
MT	Motor, see text

Chapter **14**

Introduction to stepper motors

*S*tepper motors are commonly used in robotics, automation, and positioning control in commercial and industrial equipment. If you own a computer, these motors are as close to you as your disk drive and printer. Stepper motors are used in these applications because they are easily controlled by digital circuits and, most importantly, capable of precise positioning. With this chapter, you can build a simple stepper-motor interface to examine the basic operating principles of stepper motors.

Stepper motors are different from normal electric motors. When you apply power to an ordinary motor, the rotor turns smoothly. A stepper motor however, runs on a sequence of electric pulses to the windings (or phases) of the motor. Each pulse to the winding turns the rotor by a precise amount. These pulses to the motor are often called *steps*. Stepper motors are manufactured with different amounts of rotation per step (or pulse), depending on the application it is designed and built for. The specifications of the stepper motor will state the degree of rotation per step. The range of rotation per step can vary from a fraction of a degree (i.e. 0.72°) to many degrees (i.e. 22.5°).

BASIC OPERATIONS

Figure 14-1 shows a stepper motor stepping through one rotation. Stepper motors are constructed of strong permanent magnets and electromagnets. The permanent magnets are located on the rotating shaft,

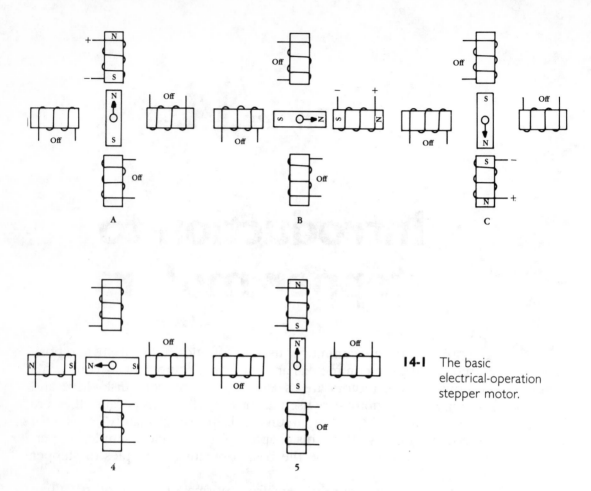

14-1 The basic electrical-operation stepper motor.

called the *rotor*. The electromagnets or windings are located on the stationary portion of the motor, called the *stator*. The stator (stationary portion of the motor) surrounds the rotor.

In FIG. 14-1 position I, look at the rotor that faces the upper electromagnet, which is on. Moving in a CW (clockwise) rotation, the upper electromagnet is switched off, as the electromagnet on the right is switched on. This moves the rotor 90 degrees in a CW rotation (shown in position II). Continuing in the same manner, the rotor is stepped through a full rotation until you reach the same position that you started in (shown in position V).

Resolution

The degree of rotation per pulse determines the resolution of the stepper motor. In the illustrated example, the rotor turned 90° per pulse, not very practical. A real-world stepper motor (for instance, one that steps 1 ° per pulse) would require 360 pulses to achieve one revolution. Another motor with less resolution (greater degree per step) that steps 3.75 ° per pulse (for example) would only require 96 pulses for one full rotation.

Without getting into gearing or gear ratios, assume that the stepper motor is used for positioning in a linear motion table, and further that each revolution of the motor is equal to one inch of linear travel on the table. It becomes apparent that each step of the motor defines a precise increment of movement.

In making a comparison between the two stepper motors, the ability to locate and position more precisely on the table would be with the stepper motor that has the higher resolution (one that requires the most steps per revolution). For the motor that steps 3.75 ° per step, the increment of movement is approximately 0.01 inch per step. If this resolution is sufficient for your table, it's fine to use this stepper motor. If, however, you needed greater resolution, the 1 °-per-step motor would give approximately 0.0027 inch per step. So, as you can see, the increment of movement is in proportion to the degrees per step.

Half step   It is possible to double the resolution of some stepper motors by *half stepping* (see FIG. 14-2). In position I, the motor starts with the upper electromagnet switched on, as before. In position II, the electromagnet to the right is switched on while keeping power to the upper coil. Because both coils are on, the rotor is equally attracted to both electromagnets and it positions itself between both positions (a half step). In position III, the upper electromagnet is switched off and the rotor completes one step. Although the figure only shows one half step, the motor can be half stepped through the entire rotation.

Other types of stepper motors

You might run across a four-wire stepper motor. These stepper motors have two coils with a pair of leads to each coil. Although the circuitry of this stepper motor is simpler than the one you are using, it requires a more complex driving circuit. The circuit must be able to reverse the current flow in the coils after it steps.

THE REAL WORLD

As stated, the stepper motors diagrammed for illustration wouldn't be of much use in the real world, rotating 90 degrees per step. Real-world stepper motors use a series of mini-poles on the stator and rotor, which improves the resolution of the stepper motor. Although FIG. 14-3 might

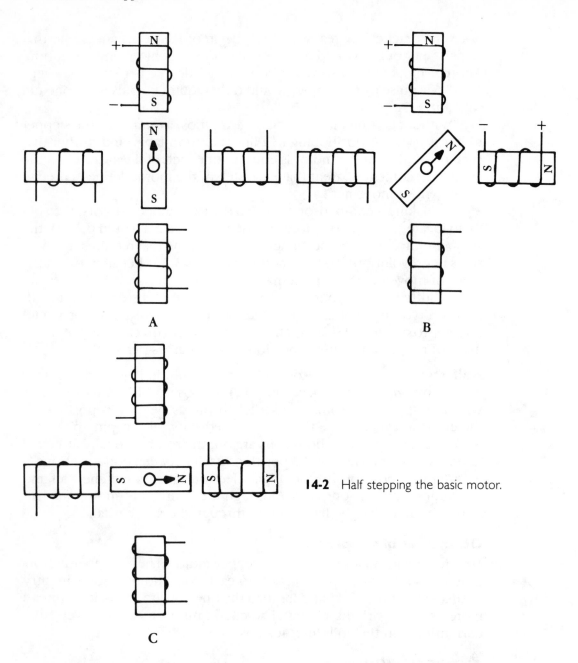

14-2 Half stepping the basic motor.

A

B

C

appear to be more complex than the previous figures, it is not really so. Its operation is identical. To prove the point, I'll step through the illustration.

In FIG. 14-3, the rotor is turning in a counterclockwise (CCW) rotation. In position I, the north pole of the permanent magnet on the

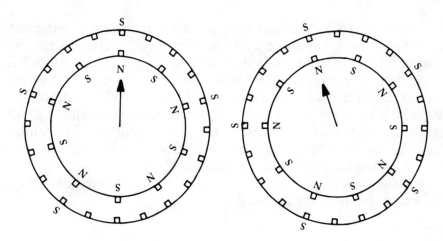

A

B

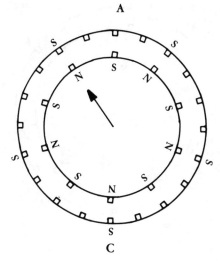

C

D

14-3 Multipole electrical-operation stepper motor.

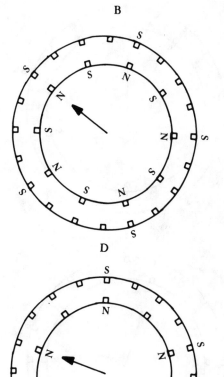

E

rotor is aligned with the south pole of the electromagnet on the stator. Notice that there are multiple positions that are all lined up. In position II, the electromagnet is switched off and the coil to its immediate left is switched on. This causes the rotor to rotate CCW by a precise amount. It continues in this same manner for all the steps. Examine the pole relationship between positions IV and V. The rotor is still moving CCW; in position V, the stator poles are in the same orientation as position I. This is where the sequence of electric pulses would begin to repeat themselves and keep the rotor turning CCW.

Figure 14-4 illustrates the half step with the multipole position. It is identical to the previously described half step.

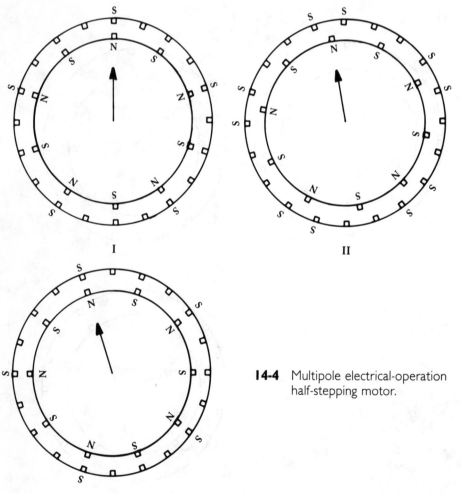

14-4 Multipole electrical-operation half-stepping motor.

TEST CIRCUIT

Although you will connect the stepper motor to a dedicated IC, I feel it would be a good idea to build a manual controller first. With this manual circuit, you can check and verify your wiring of the stepper motor before building the Amiga interface. In addition, it's an excellent tool to use if you're checking out a different stepper motor from the one used in this chapter.

Look at FIG. 14-5; the circuit is the epitome of simplicity. Switches S1 through S4 are normally open subminiature pushbutton switches (see the parts list). The four switches allow you to drive the stepper motor manually. By changing the sequence of the steps, you can do full-step and half-step increments in either direction (CW or CCW). Diodes D1 through D4 are used to prevent sparking and to protect the balance of the circuit. These diodes become more important when the motor is interfaced to a computer. The batteries used in the circuit are

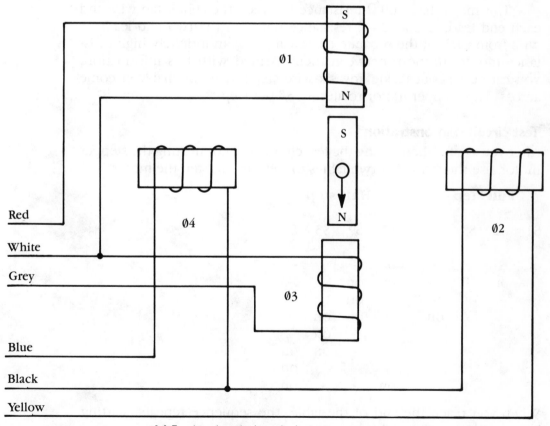

14-5 An electrical-equivalent stepper motor.

two small 12-V batteries in series to generate the required 24 V. The stepper motor is a 24-V model. The rectangular box at the top of the diagram with six screws are six PC board terminals interlocked together (see the parts list). This simplifies connecting the wiring from the motor to the circuit.

Stepper motor

Figure 14-6 is an electric equivalent circuit of the stepper motor that you are using. The stepper motor has six wires coming out from the casing (see FIG. 14-7). You can see from FIG. 14-6 that three leads go to each half of the coil windings, and that the coil windings are connected in pairs. If you just picked this stepper motor and didn't know anything about it, the simplest way to analyze it would be to check the electrical resistance between the leads. By making a table of the resistances measured between the leads, you'd quickly find which wires are connected to which coils.

This motor has a 60-Ω resistance between the center tap wire and each end lead, and a 120-Ω resistance between the two end leads. A wire from each of the separate coils will show an infinitely high resistance (no connection) between them. Armed with this information, you can just about tackle any six-wire stepper motor that you come across. This stepper motor rotates 3.75° per step.

Test circuit demonstration

After you are finished wiring the test circuit and connecting the stepper motor, use the following two tables to step or half step the motor.

Full step				Half step			
S1	S2	S3	S4	S1	S2	S3	S4
on	-	-	-	on	-	-	-
-	on	-	-	on	on	-	-
-	-	on	-	-	on	-	-
-	-	-	on	-	on	on	-
				-	-	on	-
				-	-	on	on
				-	-	-	on
				on	-	-	on

When you reach the end of the table, the sequence repeats, starting back at the top of the table.

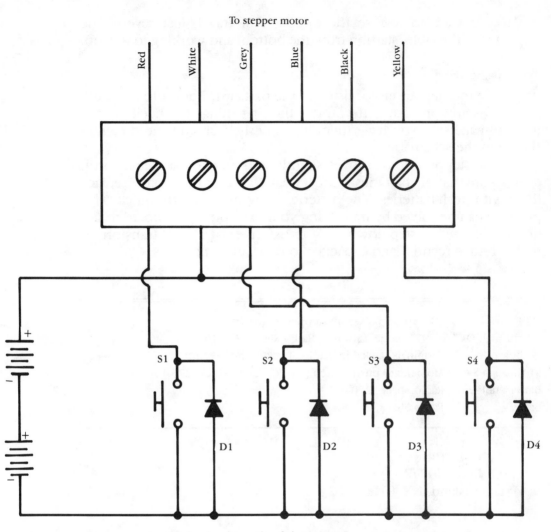

14-6 A schematic of the stepper motor.

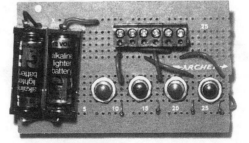

14-7 The stepper motor circuit.

If you want to reverse the direction of travel, just reverse the sequence of the table, starting from the bottom and working to the top.

Troubleshooting

If you use the stepper motor listed in the parts list, I don't think you'll run across any problems. If you do, the first things to check are the diodes; make sure you have them in properly, facing in the direction shown in the schematic.

If the stepper motor moves slightly and quivers back and forth, chances are that the batteries are too weak to power the motor; replace them with fresh batteries. The batteries do wear out pretty quick. This problem can be solved by modifying your existing circuit board to use line voltage with a step-down 12-V transformer or a 24-V transformer with a bridge rectifier and capacitor to replace the batteries.

Parts list

MT1	IM-step 3.75 six-wire stepper motor, Images Co.
D1 through D4	1N914 diode, (50/pak), Radio Shack, 276-1620
PC board	Terminals stackable, Radio Shack, 276-1388 and 276-170
S1 through S4	Momentary push switch (4/pak), Radio Shack, 275-1547
Battery holder	Radio Shack, 270-405
Battery	Radio Shack, 23-144

IMAGES COMPANY
P.O. Box 140742
Staten Island, NY 10314-0024

Chapter 15

Equatorial camera mount for astrophotography

We have all seen beautiful photographs of the night sky. Stars more abundant than you have ever seen, and some photos even show brilliantly colored gaseous nebula. The magnificence of these photos might drive you outside in the middle of the night to attempt to capture these spacescapes for yourself. You grab a tripod and your trusty 35-mm camera and you're off. What happens after the film is developed, can be to say the least, disappointing. What happened to those great photographs of the night sky?

If you anticipated that extra time is needed for the faint light of the stars to expose the film, you're right. But if you kept the camera shutter open for more than 10 seconds, the stars started to make circular trails on the photograph as a result of their apparent motion. This time restraint severely limits the quality of the photographs. Shorter exposures will eliminate the star trails, but the resulting photos will not show any nebula, and the stars will not be numerous or bright. The photographs will be rather unimpressive.

The simple equatorial mount described here will allow you to improve your night sky picture taking. With it, you can make exposures as long as 30 to 40 minutes without any star trails. These longer exposures will allow you to capture details in the night sky that you ordinarily cannot see.

The principle of the equatorial mount is simple. It moves the camera at the same rate as the stars appear to move across the sky. The apparent motion of the stars is caused by the rotation of the earth. This apparent motion of the stars across the sky is approximately 15.041° per hour. The motion of the stars will appear greatest at the horizon and least near the pole star, Polaris, in the Northern Hemisphere.

To explain this better, imagine the earth as being stationary, with the stars in the sky printed on a transparent sphere surrounding the earth (see FIG. 15-1). Now picture this transparent sphere rotating counterclockwise on a pivot point located at Polaris. You now have a pretty good mental image of how the stars move across the sky.

The type of equatorial mount that you are building is called a *barn-door mount*. These are simple mounts. Basically it is two pieces of wood, connected at the ends with a hinge, which allows the wood

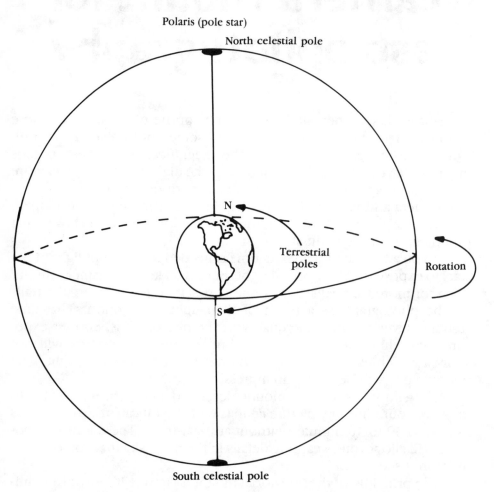

15-1 A celestial sphere, which shows Earth's rotation.

to open and close like a book. The bottom board is aligned with the star, Polaris. The top board moves upward via a drive screw, which keeps it in sync with the movement of the stars. A camera mounted on the top board tracks the stars with enough accuracy to make long exposures possible.

The advantages that this equatorial mount has over previous designs are:

- Simple electronics that control a stepper motor
- A flexible shaft that simplifies an already simple design

CONSTRUCTION

Start by cutting two pieces of ³/₄-inch-thick lumber (plywood or pressboard is fine) 8 × 12 inches to "T"-shaped pieces of wood (see FIG. 15-2). Save the scrap wood cut from these pieces and use them later.

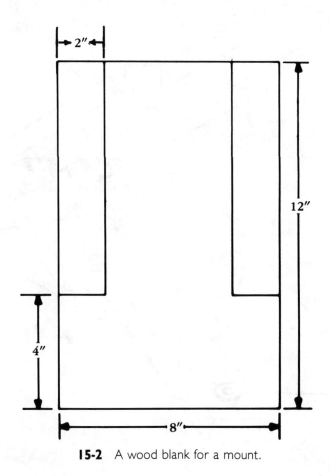

15-2 A wood blank for a mount.

Across the 8-inch dimension, join the two pieces of wood with a pair of 3-inch brass hinges. The hinges are attached so that the two wood pieces can open and close like a book (see FIG. 15-3). On one board, which will become the bottom, measure exactly 11 3/8 inches from the center pin of the hinges. Drill a hole here, centered side to side, that will accept a 1/4-20 t-nut. Hammer a t-nut into this hole, from what will be the inside when the boards are folded together. This hole is where you will place the 2 1/2-inch drive screw.

Drill another hole on the bottom board. Center this hole on the left- or right-hand side of the 8-inch section of the ''T.'' Hammer another t-nut from the inside into this hole. This hole is where you will secure the tracker to a tripod. Note: the 1/4-20 thread of the t-nut is a standard for camera tripods.

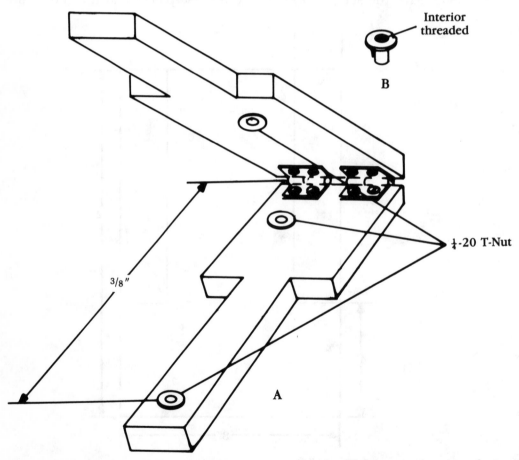

Interior threaded

B

$\frac{1}{4}$-20 T-Nut

3/8"

A

15-3 (A) The placement of hinges and t-nuts on wood blanks. (B) A perspective view of a t-nut.

Drill a hole on the top board, about 6 inches from either end, centered side to side. Hammer another t-nut in from the inside. This hole is to secure the camera to the mount.

Camera arm

The camera arm is made from one of the scraps of wood. It measures about 2 × 3 inches (see FIG. 15-4). Drill a hole on one end, through the width of the wood. In the other end, drill another hole through the thickness. Secure an "L"-shaped bracket to the t-nut on the top board of the mount. Use a 2½-inch bolt, pass it through the other side of the "L" bracket, through the hole on the width of the camera arm. Secure it with a wing nut. Use a 2-inch ¼-20 bolt and pass it through the other camera-arm hole. Secure it with a plain nut. Screw a wing nut onto the protruding bolt (as shown). The camera body is now placed onto the same bolt and locked into place by tightening the wing nut up to the base of the camera. Adjusting the wing nuts at each end of the camera arm allows you to position the camera at any desired angle.

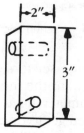

15-4 The camera arm.

The circuit

Although the circuit is simple, it is quite functional (see FIG. 15-5). There is nothing critical about the circuit; it can be hard wired on perfboard, but a PC board does help (see FIGS. 15-6 and 15-7). The circuit uses three switches: power on/off, fast/slow, and forward/reverse. The switches can be placed on the PC board, as I have done, or placed on a remote switch panel. The stepper motor is connected to the circuit using PC board wire terminals. These screw-type terminals make it easy to connect the stepper motor to the circuit. In addition, if you have a different stepper motor than the one specified, you can easily try it out in the circuit to see if it works.

When the circuit is finished, you must check and adjust its speed before attaching the stepper motor circuit to the equatorial mount.

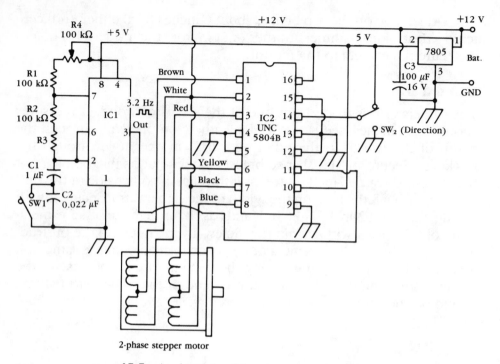

2-phase stepper motor

15-5 A schematic of the stepper motor drive.

With the speed switch set to slow mode, time one revolution of the stepper motor. You want the motor to achieve one revolution per minute. Adjust potentiometer R4 to speed up or slow down the stepper motor. The closer you get to one revolution per minute, the more accurate the equatorial mount will be. You might want to attach a wire indicator arm to the stepper motor shaft with clay or putty to make it easier to time a revolution. When you have the speed adjusted to one revolution per minute, check the forward-reverse switch and also the fast-speed setting. The use of these controls will be explained later on.

It's time to secure the circuit board and the stepper motor to the mount. The circuit is attached to the top side of the top board (see FIGS. 15-8 and 15-9). I used a few machine screws and aluminum spacers.

The stepper motor is secured to the bottom side of the bottom board (see FIG. 15-10). It is positioned on the opposite side from where the t-nut was placed for the tripod. I lowered the stepper motor from the bottom board to decrease the stress placed on the flexible shaft. Use three $2 \times 1^{1}/2 \times {}^{3}/4$-inch wood spacers, made from the scrap wood. Secure each piece of wood to the wood above it with hot glue. If you don't have a hot glue gun, epoxy will work just as well. Drill two small

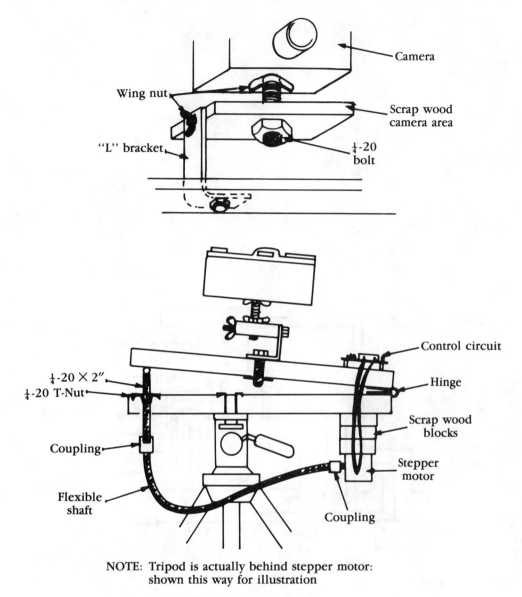

NOTE: Tripod is actually behind stepper motor:
shown this way for illustration

15-6 The PC board.

holes on the bottom board on each side of the wood blocks. Secure the stepper motor by threading wire through the holes and around the stepper motor, twist it, and tie it off. The assembly is then made more secure using hot glue (or epoxy) to hold the wire to the wood blocks and stepper motor.

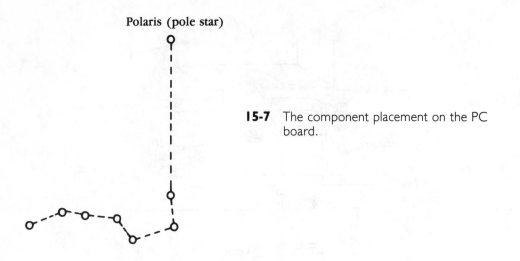

Polaris (pole star)

15-7 The component placement on the PC board.

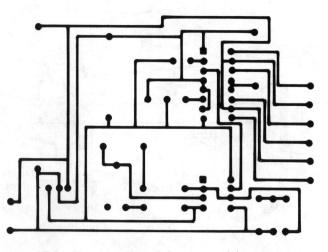

15-8 The side view of the equatorial mount.

Flexible shaft

All that remains is to attach the flexible shaft. The couplers attach the stepper motor and the 2¹/₂-inch-long driver bolt to the flexible shaft. The coupler's inside diameter is ¹/₄ inch; this diameter is fine for both the motor shaft and the bolt. The flexible shaft itself is about ¹/₈ inch diameter, so you need to use a small piece of plastic tubing over the shaft to increase its diameter before inserting it and locking it into the couplers. In a pinch, wrap electrical tape around the flexible shaft to build up its diameter.

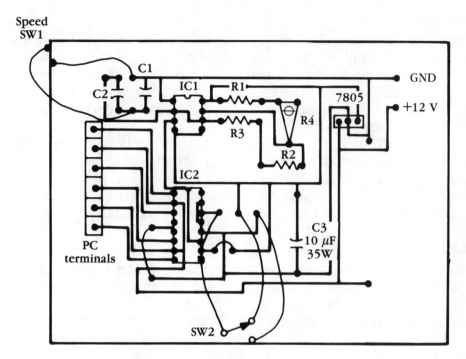

15-9 The top view equatorial mount.

15-10 The placement of the equatorial mount on the tripod and flexible shaft.

Battery

The circuit and stepper motor operates from a 12-V battery supply. You can use any 12-V battery that is capable of delivering 500 mA. Eight 1.5-V "D" cell batteries strung in series will do the trick. I used an old 12-V lead-acid car battery. Although this is a little more bulky to carry around, it drives the mount for hours without running down, and of course, it is rechargeable.

Wire a $1/8$-inch phono socket with a few inches of wire to the power-supply terminals. Solder five feet of wire to a $1/8$-inch phono plug to connect the battery power pack to the circuit. If you use a car battery as I have, you can purchase spring-loaded claw terminals from Radio Shack to connect the plug to the battery terminals.

Use

To use the equatorial mount, it must be aligned. Attach the equatorial mount to the tripod. Point the equatorial mount due North with the hinges on the left side. Now, you must align the tracker with Polaris. You can find Polaris by using the pointing stars on the front edge of the Big Dipper (see FIG. 15-11). Use the tripod to sight Polaris along the hinge pins. With Polaris sighted in this way, fasten the tripod head

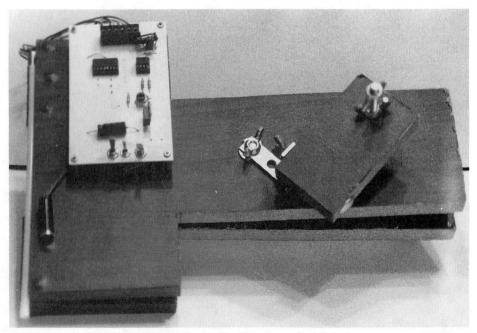

15-11 Using the Big Dipper to find Polaris.

firmly in place. You can put a small diameter tube along the hinge pins to use as a sighting tube for Polaris. I used a 2-inch piece of plastic straw.

At this point, the equatorial mount is aligned and you're ready to go (see FIG. 15-12). The driver screw should be all the way down (don't bind the drive screw into the wood, leave a $1/8$-inch clearance). The controls on the circuit should be set to a slow counterclockwise direction to slowly rise the upper board when the stepper is started. Align the camera to any area or star you want to photograph. Now, start the stepper motor. The stepper motor will turn the drive screw at one revolution per minute, this slowly lifts the upper board (and camera) in sync with the movement of stars.

I would test the equatorial mount with 1-, 2-, 3-, 4-, 5- and 10-minute exposures. Work toward longer exposures as you gain experience. You might also want to use a telephoto lens on the camera. The computer simulation on the tracker shows it to be accurate enough to use a 200-mm lens for 30 minutes. When the exposure is complete, stop the

15-12 The equatorial mount on the tripod.

stepper motor, reverse direction, and put it in the fast mode to quickly lower the board to reset the equatorial mount for another photo.

Another way to use the mount Some equatorial mounts will track more smoothly with the board moving downwards, instead of up. It's no problem to use the equatorial mount like this. Just have the hinge pins to the right when you align the tracker with Polaris. The mount should be started with the boards opened. Set the controls to turn the drive screw clockwise. Now, when you start the stepper motor, the boards will slowly close.

Film speed and aperture A large variety of films are available. Use a fast ASA color print or slide film, such as a 1600 or 3200 ASA speed. The aperture setting on the camera controls the amount of light that enters the camera. The smaller the F-stop setting, the more light that enters. You want to set the aperture to its widest opening (lowest stop number), which is usually around 2 or 2.4.

With the camera set at its largest aperture setting, the lens might not produce the sharpest picture. If you get unsharp pictures, you might need to move the stop position down to get the sharpest picture possible.

It's also a good idea to start each roll of film with a few standard photographs. This way, the photo lab that does the developing has frame markings to use. Otherwise, they might end up inadvertently cutting some pictures in half. Also tell the photo-lab to print all pictures. They might mistake your star photographs for errors and not print them.

Light pollution

If you live in or near a large city you will encounter a common problem, light pollution. I live in NYC and in the photos I took, the sky looked like dirty brown soup with a couple of stars. You have two options, take the tracker away from the city lights to shoot or purchase a light-pollution filter. Light-pollution filters are available from Orion and Lumicon (see the parts list). These filters block out the parts of the visual spectrum that are emitted by street lamps and other artificial light sources. At the same time, it allows transmission of the rest of the visual spectrum for your pictures.

Homemade light-pollution filters If you don't want to make the initial investment in a commercial light-pollution filter, you can try your hand at making one. You are restricted to using black and white film with this simple filter. Use an extreme red filter, such as a #25 or #29 filter, and place it on the front lens of your camera.

Parts list

IC1	555 timer, Radio Shack, 276-1723
IC3	7805 voltage regulator, Radio Shack, 276-1770
R1	10-kΩ resistor, Radio Shack, 271-1335
R2	100-kΩ resistor, Radio Shack, 271-1347
R3	47-kΩ resistor, Radio Shack, 271-1342
R4	100-kΩ PC-mounted potentiometer, Radio Shack, 271-285
C1	1-μF capacitor, Radio Shack, 272-996
C2	0.022-μF capacitor, Radio Shack, 272-1066
C3	100-μF capacitor, Radio Shack, 272-1016
SW1	Radio Shack, 275-634
SW2	Radio Shack, 275-635
IC2	UNC-5804B stepper controller, Images Co.
IMMT	Stepper motor, Images Co.
PCSTP	PC board, Images Co.
Flexible shaft	Images Co.
Couplers	Images Co.

IMAGES COMPANY
P.O. Box 140742
Staten Island, NY 10314
(718) 698-8305

Chapter **16**

Laser power supply for holography

*T*his chapter coincides with chapter 17. This half covers some basic concepts of holography and you can build a laser system that is capable of producing holograms. Holography can be a very simple process, which you will discover for yourself in chapter 17. You don't have to be an expert in the technical areas to shoot and develop first-rate holograms.

Holography, like photography, is a technique that produces an image on film. Holography, however, records true three-dimensional images onto film. I say "true three-dimensional" because the resulting image is not an optical illusion or trick.

Holograms record all the visual information of a three-dimensional image, including depth. Subsequently, this allows you to view the original scene from many different angles. In essence, you can look around objects in the hologram.

Holograms are becoming commonplace. If you own a credit card, chances are that it is embossed with a hologram to prevent forgery. The roots of holography trace back to 1947 when Dr. Dennis Gabor developed holography in the hopes of increasing the resolution of electron microscopes.

The evolution of the technology has been slow. Many holographic frontiers have yet to be conquered. However, holography has advanced to a point where you can use the existing technology for purely artistic pursuit.

HOLOGRAPHY VERSUS PHOTOGRAPHY

The process of holography is best understood by comparing it to photography. Photography creates a two-dimensional image on film. The film image is *a negative*. The photographic image is a single unchangeable viewpoint. The third dimension (depth) is collapsed onto the plane of the film. Figure 16-1 is a drawing of a simple box camera. The image formed by the lens onto the film is a real image. Lighting for photography can come from any number of common light sources: sun, electric lights, or flash tubes. Looking at the subject in a photograph from an angle just creates a foreshortening of the flat image, the image remains at the one viewpoint alone.

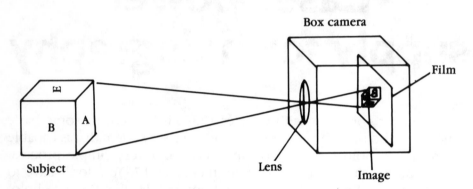

16-1 Image formation in a simple camera.

Holography does not record the subject's image the same way that a camera does. Holography records the interference pattern of light that is generated from a reference beam and reflected light from the subject (object beam). The light source required must be monochromatic (single light frequency) and coherent (wavelengths in phase). A helium/neon (HeNe) laser fits the bill.

Figure 16-2 illustrates a typical split-beam holographic setup. It is possible to produce holograms with a single beam. In fact, the holograms presented in part two of this article are single-beam setups, but in an effort to present a diagram that clearly illustrates the interference pattern created, a split-beam arrangement is better.

Holograms do not use negative to produce pictures, as in photography; the original film exposed and developed is the hologram. When finished, the hologram is a true, three-dimensional image of the subject. Figure 16-3 demonstrates the parallax of the hologram. The vertical parallax is from top to bottom, and the horizontal parallax is from left

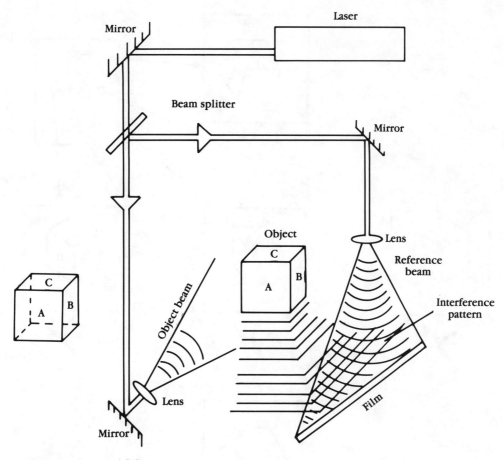

16-2 Interference pattern formation in holography.

to right. *Parallax* is a term that refers to the viewable angles of the subject in the hologram.

The two basic types of holograms are reflection and transmission. The reflection holograms can be viewed with normal white light (also called *white-light reflection*). This is the type of hologram that you can produce from information in this chapter. Transmission holograms require a monochromatic (single frequency) light source for viewing. Typically, a laser is used for illumination.

Redundancy

If a hologram is broken into small pieces, the entire image would still be viewable through any of the broken pieces. This is easier to comprehend if you look at FIG. 16-3 again. Imagine that the holographic film

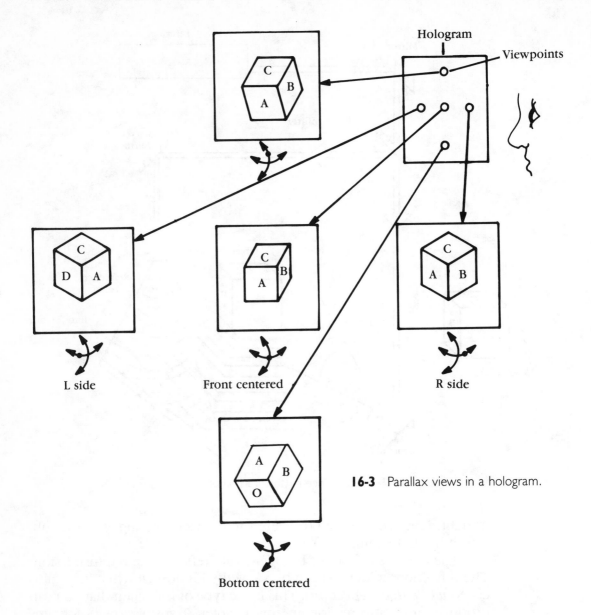

16-3 Parallax views in a hologram.

becomes a window with memory when it is exposed. So, any object behind the window, from any viewpoint, is faithfully recorded. If you covered the hologram with a black piece of paper with a peep hole in it, you could still view the entire subject through the peephole, as if you were looking through a window. Where you placed the peephole on the window (hologram) determines from which perspective you would see the subject.

Lasers

The first step in producing holograms is acquiring a suitable light source. You already know that a helium/neon (HeNe) laser fills the bill, so you need to decide either to build or buy one. Whatever your choice, the laser must meet certain specifications to be capable of producing holograms. The most important specification is that it operates in TEMoo Mode. This mode gives the most even energy distribution across the diameter of the laser beam and is critical to producing good-quality holograms.

The power of the laser is directly related to the exposure time. Shooting a hologram with a 1-mW laser will require a longer exposure time than a 2-mW laser. For beginners, either a 1- or 2-mW laser is suitable, and will keep your start-up costs down. Later, if the holography bug bites you, you can upgrade to a more powerful laser.

A 1-mW laser tube costs about $30.00; a 2-mW laser tube costs about $55.00. Laser tubes can be purchased from Allegro (see the parts list).

Laser light Before you get into the nuts and bolts of building the laser, first understand what a laser is. The following is a simplified explanation of laser function.

The word *laser* is an acronym that represents *Light Amplification by Stimulated Emission of Radiation*. Albert Einstein first theorized on stimulated emission of radiation. When an atom absorbs energy, an electron in one of its shells jumps up to a higher energy level. An atom in this state is said to be *excited*. When the electron spontaneously jumps back down to its lower energy level, it will emit a *photon* of radiation. This photon is equivalent in energy to the difference of the two energy levels that the electron jumped. If this emitted photon happens to collide with another excited atom, it will stimulate that atom to release a photon. The stimulated photon will have the same frequency and be in phase with the original photon. This is the "stimulated emission of radiation" part of the laser.

To achieve "light amplification," you need to produce a "population inversion." What this means is that you have a large number of atoms in the excited state. As a few of the atoms begin to emit photons spontaneously, they create an avalanche of photons through stimulated emission. The laser has mirrors at both ends that form an optical cavity. The photons emitted bounce back and forth between the mirrors, and produce a beam of light (through stimulated emission) that is *monochromatic* (single frequency), and in phase.

One of the mirrors that make up the optical cavity, is less than

100% reflective. This mirror allows a small percentage of light to pass through. This light is the laser beam.

LASER POWER SUPPLY

A commercial power supply for either of these tubes costs about $80.00. You can build one for less than $40.00.

Caution: the laser power supply is a high-voltage device. As with all high-voltage devices, it must be handled cautiously. The power supply should never be operated without a load connected to its output. Failure to do so will cause arcing and electrical discharge that might damage the power supply and you!

Figure 16-4 is the schematic of the power supply. The circuit is kept simple by the use of high-voltage transformer T2. The two items critical in the circuit are T1 and Q2. Transistor Q2 must be adequately heat-sinked for long continuous operation. I typically use plastic enclosures for high-voltage circuits, but I made an exception with this unit. In order to provide greater heatsinking capacity for Q2, I attached Q2 to the wall of the metal enclosure. To increase the heatsinking capacity further, I added some metal strips for additional mass.

The need for adequate heatsinking is to allow the circuit to power the laser continuously for hours without any degradation. This is critical when you want to shoot holograms. Transformer T1 provides the power to the circuit. T1 is specified in this circuit at 120 Vac/24 Vac at

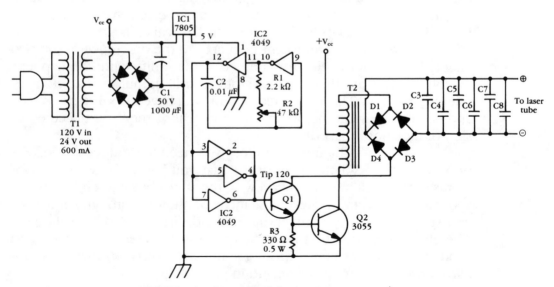

16-4 A schematic of the laser power supply.

0.6 A. This transformer is ideal for powering all laser tubes from 0.25 mW up to and including 1.5 mW. Larger transformers (higher output current) can be substituted for T1 in the circuit to power larger laser tubes, but you will have to provide greater heatsinking to transistor Q2.

The high-voltage capacitors and diodes are assembled on a separate piece of PC board. This isolates the high voltage from possibly arcing over to the oscillating section of the circuit. Be careful when working on this section of the circuit. The high-voltage capacitors can hold a voltage for a long time after the circuit is turned off. Before working on this section, short the capacitors using a wire to bleed off any charge that remains on them. Make sure that you only handle the wire by the insulation when doing this or you will get a shock.

How the supply works

The two gates of IC2 are configured as an adjustable square-wave oscillator, whose frequency is controlled by the 47-kΩ potentiometer. The output of the oscillator is buffered by three other gates on IC2. The buffered square-wave output is applied to Q1, an npn Darlington transistor, which provides a switching signal. Q1 amplifies the signal to provide sufficient current to switch Q2, a TIP3055 transistor, on and off. Transformer T2 is a high-voltage step-up auto-transformer, in series with Q2, and the switching current on its primary produces the required high voltage on the secondaries. The high-voltage output of T2 is rectified by four high-voltage diodes (D1 though D4), and filtered by six high-voltage capacitors.

Connecting the power supply to the laser

All helium/neon laser tubes require a ballast resistor to limit the current that flows through the tube. When you purchase the laser tube, be sure that you also purchase the ballast resistor. Most ballast resistors range between 50 kΩ and 200 kΩ with a 3- to 5-W capacity. The resistor generally connects to the anode (+) side of the laser tube.

It is sometimes hard to recognize the anode (+) and cathode (−) terminals on the tube. Sometimes the positive terminal is marked with an "A," a "+," or a small red dot. The negative terminal is sometimes marked with a "C" or a "K." The cathode might also be identified by a small metal tube on one end that was used to fill it with gas.

Most tubes today are hard sealed. The metal terminals on the end are also mirror mounts. The mirrors are precisely aligned to form the optical cavity. This makes it a bad idea to solder wires directly to the terminals because the heat of soldering might throw the mirrors out of

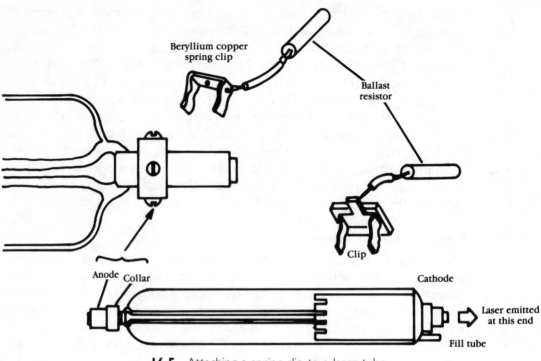

16-5 Attaching a spring clip to a laser tube.

alignment. Some companies sell beryllium copper spring clips that can clip onto the terminal. In a pinch, you can use 1/4-inch fuse clips (part number 270-739) from Radio Shack (see FIG. 16-5). The clips are attached to a bakelite base. Leave the clips attached to the bakelite and cut the bakelite in half so that you have a clip on each side. Then, bend the clip open a little to adjust it to the size of the laser terminal. Solder your lead wires to the clip, then place the clips on the laser terminals. If you are powering a laser head (a laser tube enclosed in a housing), identify the polarity by the color of the leads coming out of the housing.

Testing and calibrating the laser power supply

Never operate the laser power supply without a load connected to its output. As stated before, all laser tubes require a ballast resistor to limit the current that flows through the tube. Be sure that you have the resistor in series with the laser tube before you turn on the power supply. Failure to do so might cause permanent damage to the laser tube.

To calibrate the power supply to your laser tube, use a VOM (see FIG. 16-6). Set the VOM to read milliamps and place it in series with the laser tube. Most tubes require about 5 mA to operate. Turn on the laser

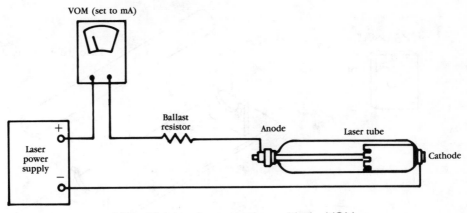

16-6 The supply connections with the VOM.

supply and adjust potentiometer R2 until the VOM reads the proper current and the laser is producing a steady beam. Use the laser beam as your final guide. The tube might require a little more current to produce a steady, unwavering beam. Allow the power supply to operate for 30 minutes or so. During this time, the components will break in. If the power output drops, readjust R2.

When you are finished adjusting the power supply, turn it off and complete the power-supply assembly. Remember that the capacitors will retain a charge for awhile. Bleed the capacitors by shorting the output leads with a wire before doing any further work.

Laser tube housing

After you have finished checking out and adjusting the power supply, you need a suitable mounting and enclosure for the laser tube. I used a laser head that has the laser tube enclosed.

Some simple mounting ideas are as follows. Locate plastic snap-in clamps (used to mount capacitors) with the same diameter as your laser tube. Mount them to a wood base and secure the laser tube in them. Another way is to get a piece of lumber, 4 × 3 × 3/4 inches thick. Drill a hole in the center of the wood that is the same diameter as the tube or laser head. Large diameter cut-out drills are available in hardware stores to drill doorknob openings. If they don't have the exact diameter you need, select the closest diameter that is a little larger. After you drill the wood, cut the wood in half so that you have two semicircles on each piece. Mount these pieces to a wood (see FIG. 16-7) with wood screws. On each side of the wood, place a wood screw. Place the laser in the wood pieces. Using #22 insulated wire, wrap the wire around the wood

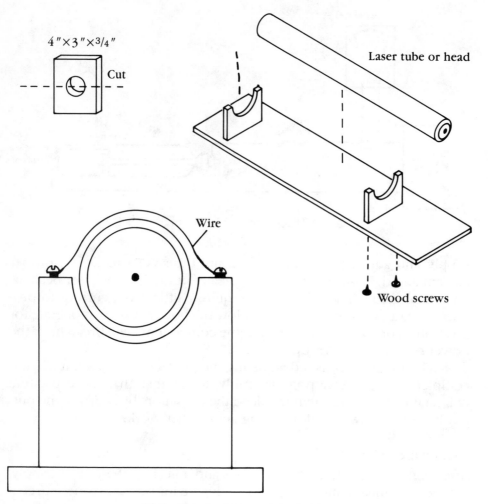

4"×3"×3/4"

Cut

Laser tube or head

Wire

Wood screws

16-7 The simple laser tube holder.

screw and lash it across the laser. Secure it to the other side using the wood screw in the same manner. Do this with both mounting pieces of wood.

If you are using an enclosed laser head, you're finished. If you are using a standard laser tube, you need to build an enclosure. The reason you need an enclosure is to prevent the glow of light from the tube from exposing the film you plan to shoot (see FIG. 16-8). Paint the inside of the enclosure black and don't forget to drill a hole in one end of the enclosure to allow the laser beam to pass through.

On another laser project, I used a rectangular aluminum pipe for an enclosure. I encountered a problem that you should be aware of.

16-8 An internal view of the laser power supply.

Because of the close proximity of the tube to the walls of the enclosure, the high voltage arced to the tube walls. I solved this problem by masking the inside of the pipe with electrical tape.

Laser safety

Never look directly into the beam of a laser. An unspread beam from a small 0.5-mW laser is well above the ANSI standard for eye safety and could cause eye damage.

Parts list

Bridge rectifier	Radio Shack, 276-1171
IC1	7805 voltage regulator, Radio Shack, 276-1770
IC2	4049 hex buffer, Radio Shack, 276-2417
Q1	TIP 120 npn, Radio Shack, 276-2068
Q2	3055 npn (TO-220 case), Radio Shack, 276-2020
C1	1000-μF 50-V capacitor, Radio Shack, 272-1047
C2	0.01-μF capacitor, Radio Shack, 272-1065
R1	2.2-kΩ resistor, Radio Shack, 271-027
R2	47-kΩ potentiometer, Radio Shack, 271-283
T1	24-V 0.6-A transformer, Mouser Electronics, 41 FK 600
T1	24-V 0.6-A transformer, Images Co.
T2	10-kV transformer, Images Co.
D1 through D4	10-kV 10-mA diodes, Images Co.
C3 though C6	6-kV 0.002-μF capacitors, Images Co.
Laser1	HeNe, 0.5 to 1 mW, Allegro, LPT-005
Laser2	HeNe, 0.5 to 1 mW, Allegro, LPT-007
Laser3	HeNe, 1 to 2 mW, Allegro, LPT-015

IMAGES
P.O. Box 140742
Staten Island, NY 10314
(718) 698-8305

ALLEGRO ELECTRONIC SYSTEMS
3 Mine Mountain Road
Cornwall Bridge, CT 06754
(203) 672-0123

MOUSER ELECTRONICS
P.O. Box 699
Mansfield, TX 76063
(800) 34-MOUSER

Chapter **17**

Holography part II

*T*he last chapter featured a HeNe laser. Now, you can continue build-ing the necessary components to shoot holograms. The first step is deciding where you can set up the equipment to shoot. The area must be quiet (no vibrations) and dark (no light). Safe lights are available so that you do not have to work in complete darkness. These lights are covered later. I usually set up my holographic equipment on the floor to reduce vibration, a concrete floor in your basement is perfect, but a bathroom or bedroom floor might be ok, too.

ISOLATION TABLE

Holograms are very sensitive to vibrations. Vibrations so subtle that you cannot feel them will prevent the hologram from forming. Because of this, holographers use an isolation table. The isolation table is designed to dampen as much vibration as possible. The table that you can build in this chapter is simple and portable. The table can be set up or stored in less than one minute.

The table consists of three components; a small piece of carpet, a small 12- to 18-inch diameter inner tube, and a metal plate (see FIGS. 17-1 and 17-2). The carpet should be large enough that the inner tube can lay on it without hanging over the edge. The inner tube has just enough air for it to be filled, but still remain very soft (in other words, you can squeeze the sides of it together easily). The top metal plate is the work-ing area and should be about the same size as the carpet. The metal

Approx. size 12″ × 14″

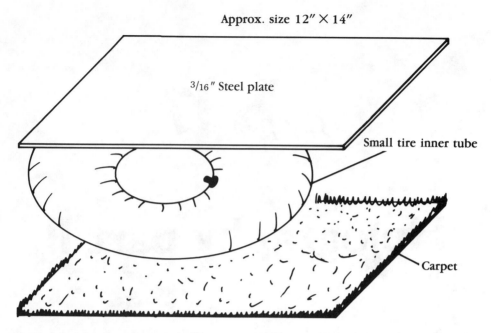

3/16″ Steel plate

Small tire inner tube

Carpet

Isolation table

17-1   The simple isolation table.

17-2   The isolation table set up to shoot holograms.

should be thick enough that it doesn't flex when components are placed on it. The plate I use is $3/16$-inch thick. If you cannot get a metal plate, you can use $3/4$ inch or thicker plywood, and adhere sheet metal to one side.

OPTICAL COMPONENTS AND MOUNTS

Keep your optical components to the bare bones minimum; use one mirror lens. The mounts for the optical components are steel plates that measure $1 \times 4^{1}/4$ inches $\times$ $1/16$ inch thick. The plates can be assembled in a variety of useful configurations using small bar magnets. I advise buying a minimum of four plates and magnets. The most basic configuration looks like an upside-down "T." Putting the plates together is simple (see FIG. 17-3). The unit is more stable than it might appear to be. When using a metal table, you can eliminate the bottom portion of the "T" and use a magnet directly on the table top.

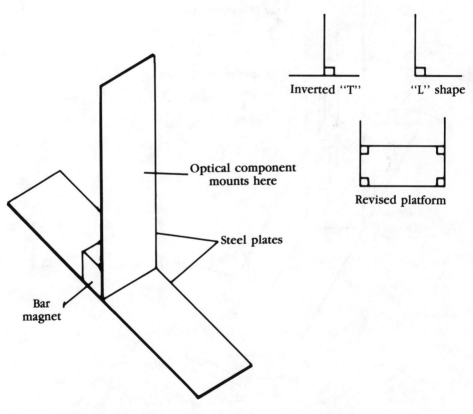

Inverted "T"   "L" shape

Revised platform

Optical component
mounts here

Steel plates

Bar
magnet

17-3 The placement of the steel plates to make the optical stand.

Securing optical components

The mirror lens is a spherical front-surface mirror attached to a bar magnet using epoxy glue (see FIG. 17-4). Be careful not to get any glue on the front surface.

With the component so mounted, it easily attaches to the side of the inverted "T," and is adjustable through a full range of motion (see FIG. 17-4). This range makes aligning and directing the laser light easy. The spherical mirror has a short focal point (see FIG. 17-5). When the laser passes the focal point it spreads rapidly and allows you to illuminate the entire photographic plate with laser light.

FILM

You could use many kinds of film to shoot holograms. My recommendation is to start with 2.5-inch square 8E75 glass plates (see the list of

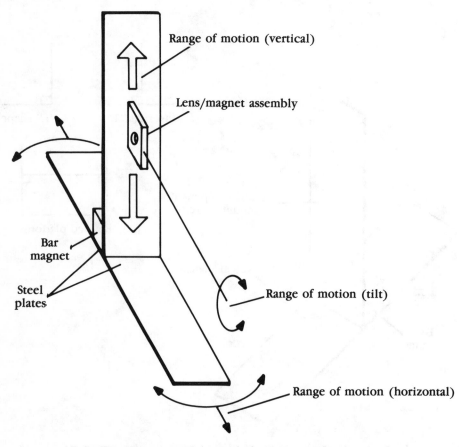

Range of motion (vertical)

Lens/magnet assembly

Bar magnet

Steel plates

Range of motion (tilt)

Range of motion (horizontal)

17-4 The placement of the optical component on the stand.

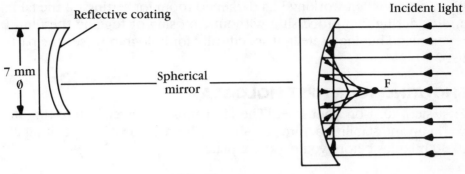

17-5 The spherical mirror.

suppliers). Using glass film plates simplifies the set-up, procedure, and the film holder itself.

Film plate holder

The film holder consists of two office binder clips with a magnet glued to each one (see FIG. 17-6). The binder clips are available from any store that sells office supplies.

SAFELIGHT

The 8E75 holographic film is least sensitive around 500 nanometers (nm) wavelength, equal to green light. A safelight provides sufficient

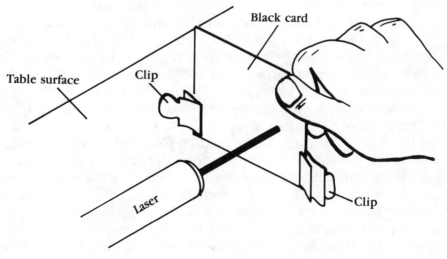

17-6 The shutter card.

illumination when working in a darkened room for setting up the table and/or during film processing without exposing or fogging the film. I recommend buying a safelight specifically for holography (see the parts list).

SHOOTING YOUR FIRST HOLOGRAM

First step, turn on your laser. The laser must be given ample time to warm up and stabilize before you shoot. The laser must be operating 20 to 30 minutes before you expose a plate.

Choosing an object

The first object you select to holograph should be smaller than the plate and should preferably be a light color; white, off white, silver, or a metallic finish. You can shoot larger and darker items later, after you gain some experience, but to start with, holograph something that will show up brightly. The object should also be rigid—something that won't flex, bend, or move during the exposure. For my first object, I chose a small white seashell.

The object must be secured to prevent it from moving or rocking during the exposure. One of the easiest ways to accomplish this is to put a small ball of clay on the table where you're placing the object. Push the object into the clay. Instead of clay, you could also use Fun-Tak™. Fun-Tak™ is a blue-colored adhesive material that has the consistency of clay. It can be pulled apart and pushed together again, rolled into balls, or whatever. The material is reusable and because of its strong adhesive properties, it is worthwhile to purchase.

Another way to secure objects is to hot glue the object to a magnet and position them with a steel plate behind the film plate. You can shoot a hologram that is viewable in white light. In addition to the materials already mentioned, you will need a white cardboard card that is the same size as a film plate, and a black card with two binding clips to block and unblock (shutter) the laser beam (see FIG. 17-6). Set up the holography table as illustrated in FIG. 17-7. Position the white card, using the film holder clips, where the film plate will be located. Adjust the mirror so that the beam reflected from the mirror is spread evenly on the white card. Remove the white card, and leave the magnet binding clip(s) in position. The laser is now illuminating the object you are shooting. Position the object close to where the film plate will be. Look at the object from the laser side; this is what your finished hologram will look like. Make any adjustments you want to the object to holo-

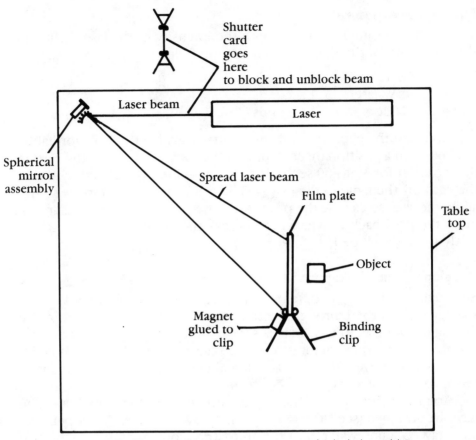

17-7 The top view of components on the isolation table.

graph it in the best position possible. Block the laser beam with the black shutter card.

With all the lights off, remove a film plate from its light-tight box. Try to hold the plate by its edges. Close the box and turn on your safe-light. The film plate appears transparent, but an emulsion is on one side. Place the plate emulsion side toward the object because this will produce a better hologram. Touch the plate with a moist finger on each side at the corner. The emulsion side is sticky. Don't worry if you can't identify the emulsion side when you first start out, you can produce a hologram with the emulsion faced either way.

Put the plate in the binding clip(s) that were holding the white card. Leave the set-up alone for a minute. This will allow any vibrations to die down.

Making the exposure

The exact exposure time varies with the intensity of the laser light and the sensitivity of the film. You can use the following times as a start.

- 1-mW laser   7 seconds
- 1.5-mW laser   4 seconds
- 2-mW laser   2 seconds

To make the exposure, lift the shutter card off the isolation table, but keep it in a position that still blocks the laser beam. Hold the card in this position for 30 to 60 seconds to let any vibration caused by lifting the card off the table to die down. Then, lift the card completely, and allow the laser to expose the plate. After the exposure time has elapsed, place the card back down, which blocks the laser beam. The plate is ready to be developed.

Developing your hologram

Although developing holograms is simple, the chemicals are poisonous and can be absorbed through the skin. Because I use my hands to move the plate from tray to tray, I always wear rubber gloves when developing holograms; you should, too. To be safe, you can also wear goggles to protect your eyes from any accidental chemical splashes, and a rubber apron to protect your clothes from stains.

You need three plastic trays large enough to hold a film plate. The trays are arranged (see FIG. 17-8). The first tray holds the developer, second tray contains water, and the third tray contains the bleach. The chemistry involved is simple, but it is easier to buy a kit than to procure the chemicals separately on your own. The kit includes pre-measured packets of chemicals that you just dump into a quart of water to make up your stock solutions. The Images Company sells an excellent developing kit (the JD-2) for $12.00. Mix the chemical according to the directions in the kit. Follow all safety precautions listed in the kit. The instructions for the kit require the chemicals to be mixed in one liter of water. For these purposes, you can substitute one quart of water for a one liter of water without any harmful effects.

Use a safelight for illumination during development. The developer is made from equal parts of two stock solutions, which are labeled A and B. Mix equal portions of the solution in the tray—just enough to cover the plate when you place it in the tray. The developing solution has a short lifetime, so mix it just before you're ready to develop the holograms. The plate is placed in the developer emulsion side up for two minutes. Gently rock the tray back and forth to keep the fresh solu-

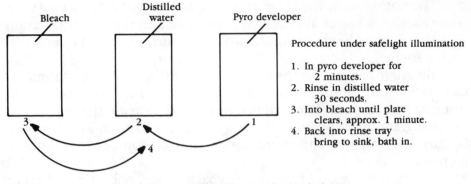

17-8 The procedure for developing holograms.

tion in contact with the plate. The plate will gather density and might appear to turn completely black. Don't worry, that's normal.

Remove the plate from the developer and place it in the water for 30 seconds. This step isn't mandatory, but it will extend the life of the bleach so that you can reuse it.

After the time has elapsed in the water, place the plate in the bleach. Rock the tray gently back and forth as before. Keep the plate in the bleach until it becomes completely clear again; this usually takes about one minute. After the plate clears, the emulsion is lightsafe, so you can turn on the room light.

Remove the plate from the bleach and put it back into the water tray. Bring the tray to a sink, run tap water at about room temperature, and place the tray under the running water for five minutes. Afterward, remove the plate, stand it vertically against a wall, and allow it to dry. The holographic image will not be visible until the hologram is completely dry.

Plates sometimes dry with water spots on them. You can dip the plate in Kodak Photo-flo solution (mix according to directions) after the final rinse to prevent water spots from forming.

Some holographers wipe the plate with a squeegee to remove excess water and thereby to speed up drying. Others use a hair dryer to shorten the drying time. If you use a hair dryer, set it on warm or low, or you might damage the hologram from excessive heat.

Viewing your hologram

After you have exposed and processed your holographic plate, it's time to take a look at your hologram. First, let the plate dry; if it's still wet, you probably won't see anything.

The hologram in the last section is a *white-light reflection*. As the name implies, it is viewable in white light. The best type of illumination for this hologram is a *point light source*. The sun is a perfect example of such a source.

Tungsten halogen lamps are an excellent light source. Incandescent lamps can be used, but the image quality isn't as good. When using an incandescent lamp, notice that if you increase the distance of the hologram from the bulb, the image appears sharper. This happens because the lamp becomes more like a point light source as the distance increases.

To improve the quality of the playback image, put a black sheet of paper behind the hologram. To make this effect permanent, spraypaint the back of the hologram black. Do this only with reflection holograms that you want to display because once it's painted, you can't use it to make copy holograms.

Real and virtual images The two types of images that you can view with your white-light reflection hologram are *real* and *virtual*. The most common example of a virtual image is the image that is reflected in a mirror (see FIG. 17-9). To the observer, the reflected rays that appear

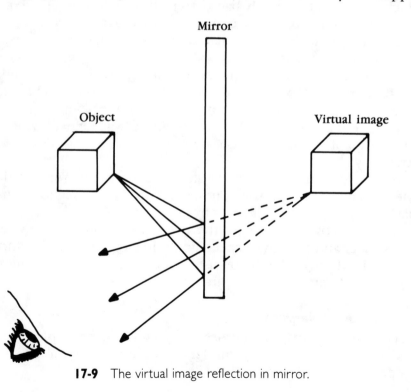

17-9 The virtual image reflection in mirror.

to come from the virtual image do not actually pass through the image. For this reason, the image is said to be virtual.

The parallax and perspective of the virtual image in a hologram is observed to be correct. As you move your head from side to side or up and down, the three-dimensional scene changes in proper perspective, as if you were observing the real physical scene (see FIG. 17-10). The virtual image is said to be an *orthoscopic image*, a true image.

In contrast to the virtual image is the real image. The real image in our reflection hologram can be observed simply by flipping the hologram around. The real image has some peculiar properties. The perspective is reversed. Parts of the image that should appear in the rear are instead in the front and vice versa. If you move your head to the right, the image appears to rotate in proportion to your movement and

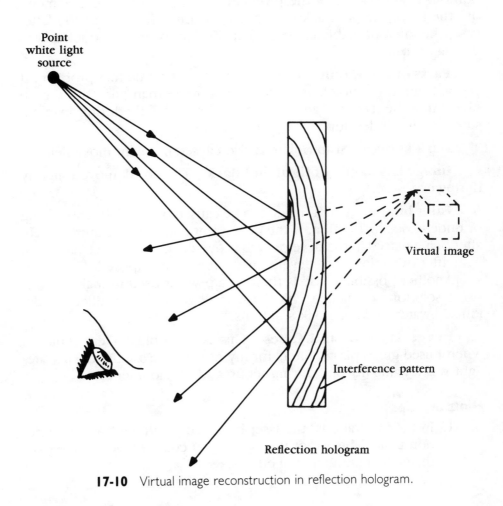

Point white light source

Virtual image

Interference pattern

Reflection hologram

17-10 Virtual image reconstruction in reflection hologram.

you see more of the left side, not the right side. The brain perceives this paradoxical visual information, and causes the image to swing around. The real image is said to be *pseudoscopic*, a false image. The real image is useful when you want to make copies of holograms. Making copy holograms is not covered in this short chapter.

Troubleshooting

Not all the holograms you shoot will be perfect. The following list will help you to locate the problem when you encounter some fault with the hologram's image.

No image   A hologram without any image can be a very frustrating problem. Even though it might seem as if you don't have a starting point to begin evaluating the problem, you do. During development, did the hologram go black or did it gain some density? In the latter case, the most probable cause is that the film plate or model moved during exposure.

Parts of hologram missing   This relates to the first problem. If you are shooting a hologram that contains more than one object, each object must be secure. If an object moves even slightly during an exposure, it will not develop a holographic image.

Dark spots   This problem is also caused by slight movement.

Image has bands of light and dark   The object moved slightly during exposure.

Faint image   A faint image can be caused by either overexposing or underexposing the film. If the plate went black almost immediately after being placed in the developer, it is overexposed. If the plate is still light after two minutes of development, it is underexposed.

Another possible cause is that the tap water used in making your stock solutions contained chlorides. If possible use distilled or deionized water for your stock solutions.

Image is weak and fades   This is a problem I encountered when I used green plastic filters for my homemade safelight. The safelight was fogging my film during set-up and development.

Hints and tips

1. In the illustrations, the laser has been positioned on the isolation table. This is not necessary, you could move the laser off the table without any ill effects.

2. Never place the power supply on the isolation table. The 60-Hz hum from the step-down transformer might cause the table to vibrate and make it impossible to produce a hologram.

3. The mixed developer (parts A and B) has a short lifetime and is not reusable. After you have successfully produced a few holograms, you might want to try batch processing. Here, you expose a few plates, keep them in a light-safe box, and develop them all at once or one after another in the same developer solution. The reason I don't advise doing this before you have successfully produced a hologram is if there is something wrong with the set-up, you'll be multiplying your errors with subsequent exposures.

4. Remember the chemicals used to develop holograms are poisonous. Always wear rubber gloves when handling or developing holograms.

Disposing of spent chemicals

The chemicals that are used to develop holograms must be disposed of after use. Check with your local sanitation department and ask for their advice. Some sanitation departments will tell you that it's alright to dispose of the spent chemicals down the drain. If that's fine, run fresh water for a minite or two after you have done so.

Other sanitation departments might advise you to take the spent chemicals to a toxic waste-disposal department or company. If this is the case, you don't want to run down there every time you develop a hologram. Store the spent chemicals in one gallon plastic jugs until they are filled, then make one trip to dispose of them. The bleach and the developer should be stored for disposal in separate jugs.

The waste water used in developing is diluted enough to dump down the drain without any problem.

One more for the road

You can create many types of holographic set-ups with the equipment you have. However, transmission holograms, copy holograms, transmission-to-reflection holograms, pseudo-color reflection holograms, and stereograms are all possible on this table.

However, try one more set-up that shows how powerful holography can be. This is called a *dual channel* or *multiplex hologram*. What you are doing is holographing two different objects onto one plate. In the finished hologram, the image changes from one to the other as your

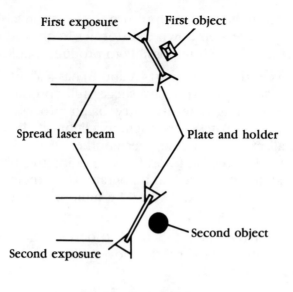

First exposure   First object

Spread laser beam   Plate and holder

Second object

Second exposure

**Double channel hologram
(multiplex)**

17-11   The procedure to make a double-channel hologram.

view angle changes. As an example, Exposure #1 could be an unopened jewelry box, and the second exposure would show the box opened, revealing an engagement ring.

One method of recording multiple images is to change the angle of the light that exposes the plate. You can accomplish this by moving the holographic plate (FIG. 17-11). The rest of the set-up is the same as was used in the reflection hologram. The exposure time for each exposure should be about half the time used to record a single hologram.

GOING FURTHER

For those of you who wish to learn more about holography and different holographic arrangements, see *Homemade Holography,* TAB Book number 3460.

Parts list

- Steel plate 1 × 4 inches × $^{1}/_{16}$ inch thick, Images Co., IM-ST
- Spherical mirror, Images Co., IM-SP
- Bar magnet, Images Co., IM-M2
- Large bar magnet, Images Co., IM-M3
- 30 pieces Agfa 8E75-HD-NAH, Images Co.

- 2.5-inch glass holographic plates, Images Co.
- Green safelite, Images Co., IM-LT
- Holographic developing kit, Images Co.

IMAGES COMPANY
P.O. Box 140742
Staten Island, NY 10314
(718) 698-8305

$Chapter$ **18**

Kirlian photography

*K*irlian photography produces strikingly beautiful photographs of the most common objects. It does so without the use of a camera or lens. The photographs are direct contact prints on film or paper using a high-voltage high-frequency power supply. Before you actually get into making Kirlian photographs, first look at some little history.

SHORT HISTORY

Kirlian photography is named after Russian researchers Semyon Kirlian and his wife, Valentina. Their work with high-voltage photography was made known in this country by a book published in 1970 titled "Psychic Discoveries Behind the Iron Curtain" by Sheila Ostrander and Lynn Schroeder.

The Kirlians claimed that this type of photography could be used as a medical diagnostic tool, stating that disease in subjects showed in photographs as a modified pattern of discharge, before obvious symptoms became manifested in the subject. Naturally, this subject generated much interest in this country. More interesting than this is a second claim known as the "phantom leaf," where a small section of a leaf is removed before photographing, but in the subsequent Kirlian photo, the missing section of the leaf appears in the photo. I have as yet to see these two claims manifested in my own Kirlian photography. I'm not saying they don't exist, just that I haven't seen them.

Although the field of electrophotography is called *Kirlian photog-*

raphy in honor of the Kirlians, the Kirlians are not the first ones to experiment with patterns created by electric discharge. The beginning of electrophotography appears to have started much sooner. Georg Christoph Lichtenberg, in the late 1700s, observed pictures made in dust created by static electricity and electric sparks.

Usefulness

It appears that there are two main avenues for development. One is to use Kirlian photography for special-effects photographs. You can add the equipment and technique to your repertoire of photography. The other is to investigate the potential of this method of photography for its scientific value. You can experiment with Kirlian photography and attempt to verify some of the claims.

Debunking the myths

Kirlian photography has the potential to become a scientific instrument. Notice the operative word "potential" in the last sentence. Despite any claims to the contrary, this type of photography cannot, as of yet, be used for any medical diagnostic purposes. Any and all research I have read to date draws inconclusive results. It appears that the patterns and "aura" of these electrophotographs are determined by the conductivity of the object, the pressure on the plate, and the moisture content of the air. Anyone claiming otherwise is, at this point in time, perpetrating a fraud.

Herein lies the key for doing legitimate research. By controlling the variable factors mentioned: conductivity, pressure, and humidity, as well as frequency of discharge, duration of exposure, and using a measured and controlled high-voltage source, you can begin to lay a foundation of research. Kirlian photography has already been shown to be useful for some types of nondestructive testing.

Cold electron emission

The high-voltage potential causes a cold electron emission that is rich in ultraviolet light. As far as I know, no one has done any UV spectrographic testing of this light. This might be another area for research.

CIRCUIT OPERATION

TR1 is a stepdown transformer that brings the line voltage down to 25.2 Vac (see FIG. 18-1). The power from the transformer is rectified by RECT and C1. IC1, a 7805 voltage rectifier, provides +5 V to IC2, a 4049 hex inverter. Two gates off the inverter are set up as an adjustable

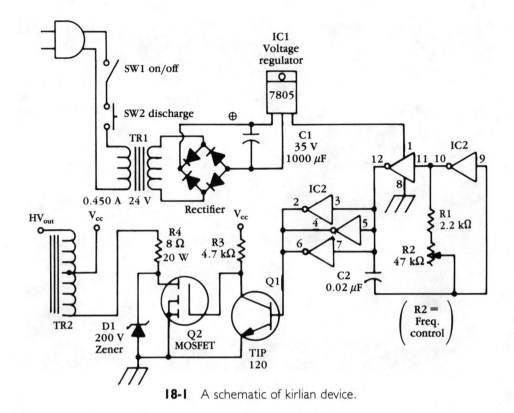

18-1 A schematic of kirlian device.

oscillator, using C2, R1, and R2. The oscillator is adjustable, using R2, from approximately 500 to 10,000 Hz. The output of the oscillator is fanned into three gates on the 4049 in parallel. The output from the three gates provides sufficient current to trigger Q1, a TIP 120 npn Darlington transistor. Transistor Q1, in turn, triggers Q2, a high-powered MOSFET. D1, a 200-V zener diode, protects the MOSFET from reactive voltage surges by providing a clean path to ground. Resistor R4 provides current limiting through the MOSFET.

CIRCUIT CONSTRUCTION

Basically Kirlian photography is a high-voltage contact print of an object. The device outlined here provides the high-voltage source needed to produce the photographs. The circuit is pretty simple, so you can use point-to-point wiring (see FIG. 18-2).

The high-voltage transformer used in the circuit is an auto-transformer that has three electrical leads. The two wires on the side are where power is supplied by the circuit. The center terminal, the green

18-2 The internal view of a kirlian device.

insulated wire, is the high-voltage terminal. Strip about 1¹/₂ inches of insulation from this wire to connect it to the exposure plate.

The housing can be any nonmetallic case made of plastic or wood that is large enough to house the components. Use a panel-mounted "normally open" momentary contact switch to control exposure. The exposure plate and the controls are placed on top of the enclosure (see FIGS. 18-3 and 18-4).

Exposure plate

The plate is the next most important item after the circuit. The plate is constructed from a 4-×5-inch single-sided piece of copperboard. A ¹/₂ to 1 inch border is stripped of copper, using a ferricchloride etchant kit, which is available from Radio Shack.

The border helps prevent electrical arcing from the bottom side (copper side) of the board to the top when making photographs. This border also makes it safer to photograph human subjects.

You can purchase the plate with a stripped border (see the list of suppliers) or you can make the plate yourself.

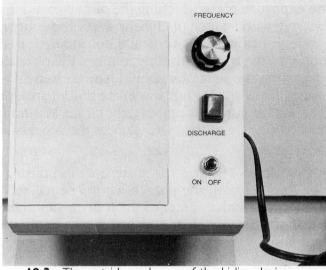

18-3 The outside enclosure of the kirlian device.

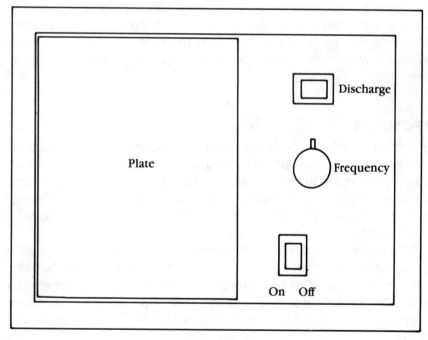

Kirlian device

18-4 A kirlian device.

Making the exposure plate   Etching the plate is easy. Fill a small plastic or rubber tray with 1/2 inch of etchant. Place the copper plate in the tray on its side so that it stands vertically up. Secure it in this position for 20 minutes. At the end of this time, remove the plate and rinse it in running water from the sink. You should have a 1/2-inch border that is clean of copper. If any copper remains in the border area, put the board back in the solution until it is completely clean. You now have a 1/2-inch border on one side of the plate. Repeat the process for the other three sides.

Mounting the plate   Position the plate on the housing where you want it to be located. Mark the corners with a pencil and remove the plate. Find the approximate center of the four corner marks and drill a 1/4-inch hole in the housing.

Reposition the plate back on the top of the housing, and use the four corner marks as a guide, copper side down. Mark the location of the drilled 1/4-inch hole on the copper side, using a pencil from the other side of the housing.

Remove the plate and solder a wire in the center of your pencil mark on the copper side. Then, secure the plate to the top of the housing permanently. Position the plate with the copper side down, with wire going through the drilled hole in the housing. Then, glue it into place using epoxy or hot glue. When the glue has dried, connect the end of the wire from the copper plate to the high-voltage wire on the transformer.

EXPOSURES

Depending on what you are photographing determines whether or not the object should be grounded. Grounding an object intensifies the discharge. However, you should only ground inanimate objects. If you are photographing a living subject, such as yourself or a pet, under no circumstance should that subject be grounded or be allowed to touch a ground during exposure—this will lead to a nasty shock.

When photographing an inanimate object (such as a leaf, a coin, or keys), connect the object to a ground to get a better picture. You do this by connecting a wire to an earth ground, such as a water pipe, then to the object that you are photographing. In a pinch, you can eliminate the ground wire and just touch the object with your finger during exposure.

Exposures are usually made in complete darkness, unless you are using specially packaged film (see the index of suppliers). If you use unpackaged film, you can let a tiny amount of light in—just enough to see what you're doing. I have done so when shooting a few Kirlian photos. So far, this light hasn't fogged any photos.

Allow a minute or two for your eyes to become accustomed to the darkness. Place the film emulsion side up on the exposure plate (the emulsion is the shiny black side of the film). The film usually has a nick or mark in one of its corners. If you place the nick on your right-hand side, the emulsion side of the film will be facing you. Put the film on the discharge plate with the nick on the right-hand side. Place the object you are photographing on the film. If the object is inanimate, connect a ground wire to it. Turn on device and press the discharge button for 5 seconds, making the exposure.

The exposure time is determined by trial and error. Start with 5 to 10 seconds, and adjust it accordingly. The frequency of the discharge can also be varied to get different discharge effects.

Film

You can use just about any kind of paper or film to shoot Kirlian photographs. I recommend using 4-×5-inch transparency film, either tungsten balanced or daylight (see FIG. 18-5). Both types of film give striking

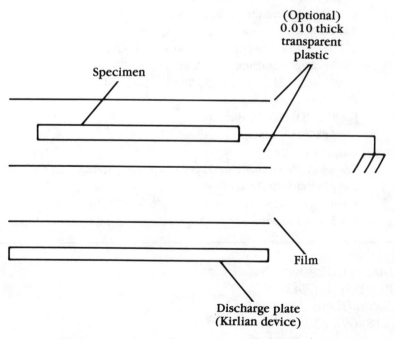

18-5 A specimen placement on a discharge plate.

color transparencies. Tungsten-balanced film gives colors that range in the yellows, oranges, and reds. Daylight film colors range mostly in the greens and blues.

Shielded film   Individually wrapped 4- × 5-inch sheet film is available for shooting Kirlian photographs in daylight. The film is enclosed in sealed black plastic. A notch in the plastic is kept on the right-hand side when it is placed on the device's discharge plate. This orientates the emulsion side of the film facing up. The object is placed on the film and exposed, as before. The film is brought to a photolab, where it is removed from the plastic under light-tight conditions and is developed.

Parts list

TR1	120-Vac/25.2-Vac 450-mA transformer, Radio Shack, 273-1366
SW1	Momentary contact, normally open, Radio Shack, 275-1571
SW2	SPST 120-Vac switch, Radio Shack, 275-651
RECT	50-V 1-A rectifier, Radio Shack, 276-1185
C1	1000-μF 35-V capacitor, Radio Shack, 272-1032
C2	0.022-μF 50-V capacitor, Radio Shack, 272-1066
R1	2.2-kΩ 1/4-W resistor, Radio Shack, 271-1325
R2	50-kΩ potentiometer, Radio Shack, 271-1716
R3	4.7-kΩ 1/4-W resistor, Radio Shack, 271-1330
R4	8-Ω 20-W resistor, Radio Shack, 271-120
Q1	TIP 120 npn Darlington, Radio Shack, 276-2068
IC1	7805 voltage regulator, Radio Shack, 276-1770
IC2	4049 integrated circuit, Radio Shack, 276-2449
TR2	HV transformer, Images Co.
Q1	IRF830 MOSFET, Images Co.
D1	1N5388 200-V zener, Images Co.
PC board	Images Co.
Misc.	4- × 5-inch individually packaged color transparency film for daylight Kirlian photography, Images Co.
	Plastic instrument enclosure, 6.25 × 6 × 3.25, Images Co.
	4- × 5-inch copper-clad board striped with 3/8-inch border, Images Co.

IMAGES COMPANY
P.O. Box 140742
Staten Island, NY 10314
(718) 698-8305

Chapter  **19**

Pinhole photography

P_inhole photography_ is a fascinating subject. The idea that a small hole, a pinhole in fact, can project an image onto a plane is amazing (see FIG. 19-1). The cost of making a pinhole camera is minimal—a few dollars at most, depending on your resourcefulness. The camera described here was built for less than one dollar.

HISTORY OF PINHOLE OPTICS

Who was the first to discover that a pinhole could project an image? Photographic folklore is a little fuzzy; some attribute the discovery to the Arabs, others to the Greeks.

Leonardo Da Vinci however described the principles of pinhole optics and made sketches for a ''camera obscura.'' The word _obscura_ literally translated means ''darkroom.'' The camera obscura is a darkroom with a pinhole that projects an upside-down view of a scene outside of the room. Artists could trace these projected images onto paper or canvas and use the sketches for paintings. This was before photosensitive materials were discovered to create pictures.

During the 16th century, portable camera obscuras were used by artists to capture scenes at different locations. The 17th-century Dutch painter Vermeer is believed to have used a camera obscura for many of his paintings.

In 1568, a quantum leap in camera obscura technology was instituted when Danielo Babarbo of Padua suggested using a lens in place of the pinhole. Thus, the outline for a modern camera was complete.

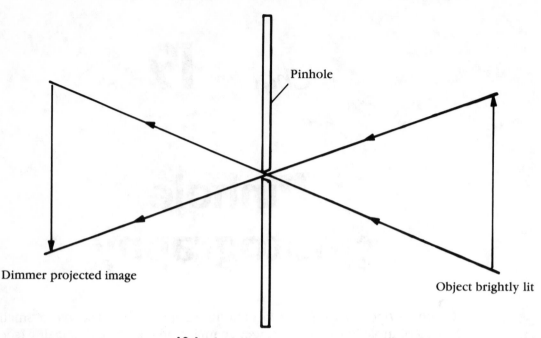

Pinhole

Dimmer projected image

Object brightly lit

19-1   A pinhole image formation.

PINHOLE CAMERA

A pinhole camera can be made from just about any light-tight box or can. The size of the box determines the size of film or paper you can use inside of it. I built a camera out of a discarded circular cookie can. This is an example, just remember you can substitute any other light-tight box or can to your liking.

The circular can measures 7 inches in diameter and 3 inches in height (see FIG. 19-2). Drill a 1/4-inch hole in the side where you will be placing the pinhole. Paint the inside of the box flat black to prevent any internal reflections. Paint the outside of the box white. The outside is painted white to prevent heat building up inside the can when you are in a sunny location.

On the side opposite the 1/4-inch hole, glue two film holders (see FIG. 19-2 and FIG. 19-3). The film holders can be fashioned from any suitable material, cardboard, plastic, or wood. I used two wood popsicle sticks cut in half. Locate the film holders by first drawing an imaginary line from the 1/4-inch hole directly across the can or box. This is the center point of the film holder.

Use a piece of film or paper that you plan to use in the pinhole camera to mark the placement of the film holders. I used a 5-×7-inch

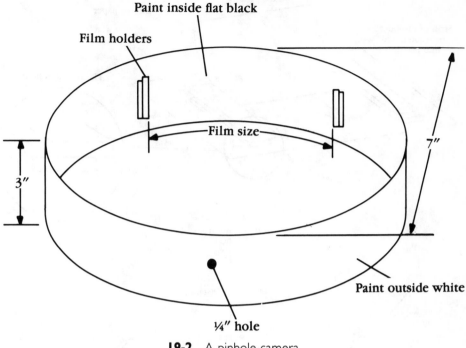

Paint inside flat black

Film holders

Film size

7″

3″

¼″ hole

Paint outside white

19-2 A pinhole camera.

black and white paper in this camera, cut in half to 2.5 × 7 inches. I removed one sheet of film from the box, (use a darkroom, don't open paper in daylight) and used this one sheet of paper to mark where the film holders should go. Hold the paper at its center point in line with the imaginary line from the 1/4-inch hole. Mark the can at each end of the paper. You could, of course, measure the distance from the center point to each side. However, this is an easy way to make a mistake—especially if you're working on a curved surface. When you're finished marking the box, discard the paper; if it has been exposed to daylight, it is no longer any good.

Next, glue in the bottom strip of the film holder. Move the bottom strips out slightly, and make the holder a little larger than what you marked. This will prevent the film from binding or bowing outward when film is placed inside. When the glue dries, secure the top strips.

The pinhole

The pinhole is the most critical piece of the camera (see FIG. 19-4). Make your pinhole with a standard hand sewing needle. Needles are available in different sizes (different diameters). The following list

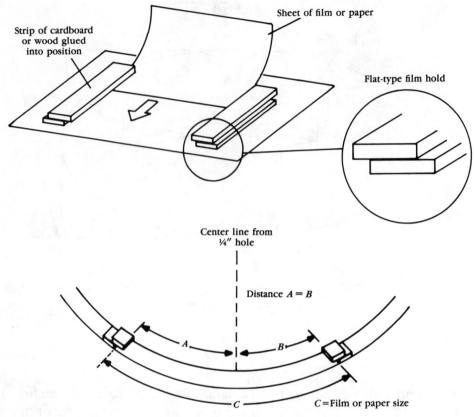

Sheet of film or paper

Strip of cardboard or wood glued into position

Flat-type film hold

Center line from ¼″ hole

Distance $A = B$

A B

C $C =$ Film or paper size

19-3 Making a film holder.

compares the needle number to its diameter and the optimum focal length for that particular diameter. The focal length corresponds the distance from the pinhole to the film or paper.

Needle number	Pinhole diameter	Focal length	Approximate F-stop
14	0.012	3″	250
10	0.018	4.5″	250
9	0.021	6″	280
8	0.024	8″	325
7	0.027	10″	375
6	0.030	12″	400
5	0.033	14″	425
4	0.036	16″	450
3	0.039	20″	500

19-4   An internal view of a pinhole camera.

This information is to be used as a guide, it is not written in stone. For instance, I have used a 0.018-inch pinhole with a focal distance of 7 inches.

F-stop

There's an easy way to figure out the F-stop for any pinhole and focal length. F-stop=Focal length/pinhole diameter. For my camera, this works out to 7/.018=388, so the F-stop is 388. Why would you want to know the F-stop of your camera? The figure will help you set the exposure for your film. This is covered later.

Making your pinhole

To make your pinhole, you need a needle, piece of fine aluminum-grit sandpaper, and a piece of cardboard. If you don't have one of the specified needles, use the smallest sewing needle you have, it'll probably work.

You could use a piece of aluminum foil, but it is a little too thin. It's better to use a piece of aluminum from a disposable baking pan, which is available in the housewares department of your local supermarket. A piece of steel or brass shim stock is also a good choice, if it's available. An appropriate thickness is 0.003 inch.

Cut a 1-inch square from your aluminum or shim stock. Place it on top of the cardboard or paper. Push the needle through the metal sheet by about $1/8$ of an inch, and rotate the needle (see FIG. 19-4).

Remove the needle and turn the metal sheet over. Take the fine sandpaper (600 wet/dry) and gently sand the surface to remove any burrs. Then, gently reinsert the needle to remove any debris. Hold the pinhole up to the light to examine it.

Finishing the camera

Tape the pinhole on the inside of the can or box so that it lies in the center of the $1/4$-inch hole that you drilled. The shutter is very simple. If you are using a metal can as I did, place a small magnet over the $1/4$-inch hole (see FIG. 19-5). This is your shutter. If you are using another material, tape a black piece of construction paper over the $1/4$-inch hole to form a shutter. Your camera's finished. Before you start taking pictures, get a small pinhole darkroom set up.

PINHOLE DARKROOM

In a pinhole darkroom, you don't need an enlarger. What you do need is an area that is relatively light tight. In many cases, a home bathroom or closet can be used, just stuff a towel by the bottom of the door to block any light from entering.

I recommend using paper in your camera instead of film. With

19-5 A pinhole camera.

paper, safe lights are available that will not fog the paper. This allows light for you to work in your darkroom, for developing, or to load and unload the camera. In the case of my camera, I needed to cut the 5-×7-inch paper in half, to 2.5×7 inches. This task would have been much more difficult if I had to work in complete darkness. With film you have no choice; you must work in complete darkness.

If you follow my suggestion, the second item you need is a safe light. The type of paper you use determines what safe light you need. I recommend you use RC poly-contrast Kodak black-and-white paper. For this paper, an OC-filtered (light amber) safe light is recommended. In a pinch, try a 7-W red bulb or red cellophane wrapped around a clear 7-W bulb.

Loading the camera

Under the safe light, remove a sheet of photographic black-and-white paper from its box. Examine the paper. One side is glossy, the emulsion side. The other is a flat white, possibly with the manufacturer's print on it. Load the camera with the emulsion side of the paper facing the pinhole.

Exposure

Exposure is determined by four factors: intensity of light, aperture (F-stop), time (shutter speed), and emulsion sensitivity.

Light   Shoot only during daytime using sunlight to begin. Later, as you gain experience, you might want to try indoor shooting, but this will probably require you to change to film instead of using paper.

Aperture   This is the simple F-stop calculation used when making the pinhole.

Emulsion   The paper emulsions that you are using typically have an ISO 4 speed. Films are much faster, up to ISO 3200. This speed would cut exposure time considerably.

Time   This is the shutter speed. If you like, you can ignore all calculations and make a 2-minute exposure. When developing the paper, you can determine if you should increase or decrease your shutter speed.

Figure 19-5 illustrates the aperture opening, as compared to the F-stop number. The larger the F-stop, the smaller the opening. Each progression of the F-stop number reduces the light intensity that reaches the film by 1/2. Most 35-mm cameras today either have auto-exposure or in-camera light metering. You can use a trick that was devised for use in case of light meter failure. For taking a bright sunlit picture, set your aperture to F/16 (F-stop 16) and your shutter speed equals the ISO rating of your film. So, if you were shooting ISO 200 film, your shutter speed would be 1/200 of a second. Now, if you increased the F-stop to F/22, you would decrease the light intensity by 1/2. To get the correct exposure, you would need to double the exposure time and set the shutter speed to 1/100 second.

You are using paper that has the approximate ISO speed of 4. So, at F/16, you need a 1/4 of a second exposure. Pinhole cameras have relatively high F-stop numbers. The calculation for my camera is F/388. Looking at the following information, you see that this F-stop is pretty close to the F/360 at 128 seconds. So, my exposure time for this particular camera is 2 minutes. Use the calculated F-stop for your camera and use the following information to approximate an exposure.

F-stop	Exposure time
2.8	1/128
4	1/64
5.6	1/32
8	1/16
11	1/8
16	1/4
22	1/2
32	1
45	2
64	4
90	8
128	16
180	32
256	64
360	128
512	256

Simple development

You are using standard photographic developing chemistry, so follow all safety recommendations that are listed on the packages. At minimum, you should wear gloves to prevent getting any chemicals on your skin, and possibly goggles and an apron, depending on your experience and comfort level working in a darkroom. If you are working with paper, you can develop the paper using the safe light.

You need four trays that are large enough to hold the paper you are using (see FIG. 19-6). The temperature required for the chemicals is very forgiving, room temperature is fine, but anything between 65 and 80 °F will do.

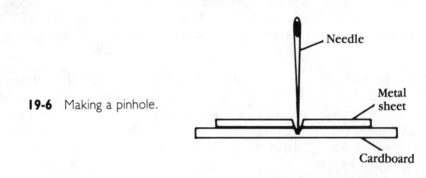

19-6 Making a pinhole.

Needle

Metal sheet

Cardboard

Hold needle straight, press down and rotate

Tray 1 contains a *developer*; you can use just about any development, mix according to directions on the package. Most developers require about 2 minutes. You can gauge your exposure by how the picture looks after development. If the paper has a light or faded image, it is underexposed—it needs a longer exposure in the camera. If the paper turns very dark or completely black, it is overexposed—too much light cut the exposure time in the camera.

You can compensate for underexposures or overexposures somewhat by varying the time in the developer. For an underexposed paper, keep it in the developer another 2 minutes or until it reaches a density that you like. After about 4 minutes, the developer isn't going to do much more. With overexposed paper, if the paper is turning black, remove it immediately and put it into the stop bath, this might salvage the print. Proceed with the balance of development. Although you might salvage some prints this way, it's a good idea to learn from the experience. Vary your exposure time in the camera accordingly.

Tray 2 contains a *stop bath*. This, as the name implies, stops further development. You can buy a commercial stop bath or use plain water. A stop bath is better, and it helps prevent the fixer from being contaminated with developer solution. The 30-second time is a minimum; you could leave the print in the stop bath longer.

Tray 3 contains the *fixer*, this solution fixes the image on the paper so that it is no longer light sensitive. After the paper has been in the fixer for 2 minutes, you can turn on a regular light. The 2-minute time is a minimum, you could leave the print in the fixer for a much longer time.

Tray 4 contains water, it is a holding tray. It holds the prints in water until you can take it to running water. After you are finished with all the prints you are developing, place the tray under running water for 30 minutes or so. This removes the fixer from the paper. If the fixer isn't removed, it will eventually turn the print brown and fade the image.

The paper negative If you just finished processing a picture from your camera, you might be surprised to find that it's a negative. You might be a little wary at this point wondering how good a picture you can get from a paper negative (I know I was). Rest assured, the results are very good. You will not be able to tell that the picture was made from a paper negative and not a film negative. After processing the paper, you can immediately make a contact print before you store the developing chemicals.

If the paper negative you just developed is still wet, that's ok. Under safe-light illumination, remove a fresh sheet of paper from its box. Wet this paper with water. Place the papers together, emulsion to emulsion, with the negative on top. Put the papers down on a flat surface. Turn on the room light for 1 second. Now develop the fresh sheet of paper and you will have a positive print (see FIGS. 19-7 and 19-8).

You could also do this with dry paper. If you want to try it, put a clean piece of glass on top of the sandwich to hold the papers flat. Always make sure the negative is on top or you won't get a picture. You can vary the 1-second exposure, depending if the positive is underexposed or overexposed.

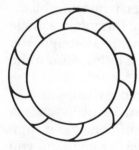

F-stop 2.8

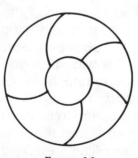

F-stop 11

F-stop 22

19-7 F-stop and aperture size.

Tray 1	Tray 2	Tray 3	Tray 4
Developer time 2 minutes	Stop bath 30 seconds	Fixer time 2 minutes	Water (see text)

19-8 The procedure for developing.

19-9 A paper negative.

19-10 A paper positive.

GOING FURTHER

This chapter is restricted to using paper in the pinhole camera. After you have gained some experience, you might want to try your hand using film. Color transparency, print, and black-and-white sheet film is available in a 4-×5-inch size. The disadvantage to using film is that it must be loaded and unloaded in the camera in total darkness. It also must be developed in total darkness.

The advantages are the ability to take color pictures using much shorter exposures. As a guide, when you double the ISO speed of the film, you decrease the exposure time necessary by $1/2$. The following information will put you in the ballpark in regard to exposure times for various film speeds.

ISO multiply exposure time

ISO	multiply exposure time
4	1
8	0.5
16	0.25
32	0.12
64	0.06
125	0.03
200	0.015
400	0.008
800	0.004
1600	0.002
3200	0.001

As an example, for the camera illustrated here, if the camera was loaded with ISO 64 film, you would multiply the 128-second exposure by 0.06. So $128 \times 0.06 = 7.68$ seconds. That is rounded off to 8 seconds to make the exposure.

Chapter 20

Oil and gas from coal

*T*he days of coal-driven locomotives and sea-faring ships have passed. Even so, coal can still be exploited to provide fuel for today's contemporary cars and home heating systems. Coal can be converted into synthetic gasoline and oil.

The principles of this technology have been in existence for quite a few years. In fact, the conversion of coal into illumination, cooking, and heating gas was an established commercial technology here in the United States in the 1820s. With the advent of cheaper natural gas and its greater heating value, coal gas quickly disappeared.

The heating value of coal gas ranges from 125 to 560 British Thermal Units (BTUs) per cubic foot, depending on the grade of the coal used and the temperature. Natural gas has a heating value of 1,030 BTUs. The gasification of coal produces a gas that is a mixture of methane, hydrogen, and carbon monoxide.

SYNTHETIC GASOLINE AND OIL

The conversion of coal into oil and synthetic gas has not been pursued in the United States on any large scale. However, large-scale operations existed in Germany during World War II. The Germans produced 12,000 barrels of synthetic gas from 600 tons of coal per day.

The conversion of coal into oil and gas requires the adding of hydrogen to the coal. The ratio of hydrogen to carbon in coal is approximately 0.8 to 1. In oil, this ratio is 1.75 to 1.

In large syn-gas plants, water can be used as a source of hydrogen, in the form of high-temperature high-pressure steam. To make this process economical, the energy to super heat the water to derive the hydrogen from steam must be supplied from the coal.

MAKING FUEL GAS FROM COAL

Numerous ways are possible to generate gas from coal. The simplest method is *nondestructive distillation* by heating the coal in the absence of oxygen (air). When performing this experiment, wear safety goggles.

Figure 20-1 details the simple fuel-gas generator. The reaction vessel is a test tube with a rubber stopper. A short section of glass tubing goes through the stopper to a simple air valve used in home aquariums. The valve is kept open during gas generation, which allows the gas to collect in a bag. Heat the coal gently and evenly when you first begin. As the gas generation starts, you can heat more safely without worrying about the test tube shattering or exploding. When the gas generation is complete, the valve is closed and the gas generator is removed from the valve and replaced with a simple burner, fashioned out of glass or brass tubing (see FIG. 20-2). With the burner connected, open the air valve and apply gentle pressure on the gas collection bag. Hold a match by the burner tip to ignite the escaping fuel gas.

Buying coal

Coal can be purchased from any store that sells barbecue supplies. Coal that is intended for a barbecue works quite well in our generator. Crush

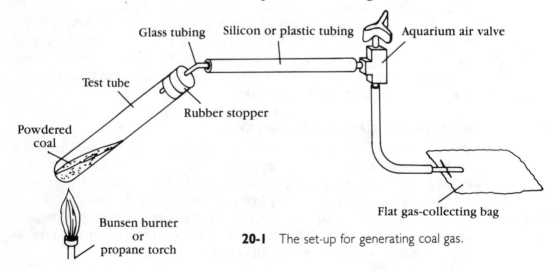

20-1 The set-up for generating coal gas.

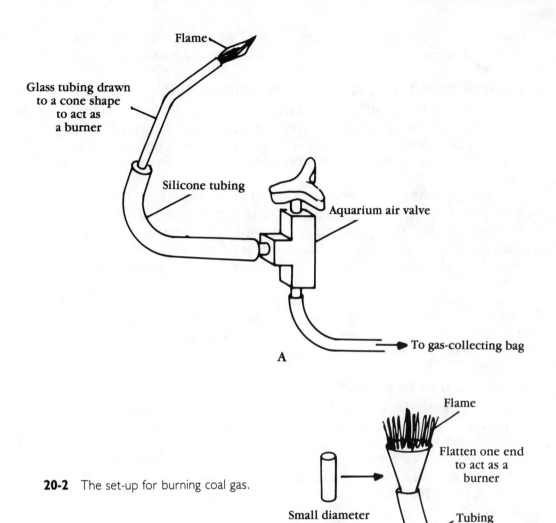

20-2 The set-up for burning coal gas.

the coal into a powder before using it in the reaction vessel. Do not use any type of carbon material from aquarium supply stores. Although this material looks like coal, it will not work.

Caution

Coal gas, as explained earlier, contains carbon monoxide and hydrogen. Both these components have a heating value of 300 BTUs per cubic foot. Unburned carbon monoxide is poisonous. Although the small amount produced in this generator is not dangerous, if the process is scaled up it does become an important consideration.

MAKING SYNTEHTIC GAS AND OIL FROM COAL

This process is beyond the reach of the amateur scientist at this point in time, but this doesn't prevent you from examining the process. The residue that is left in the test tube from the fuel-gas experiment is the raw material needed for making synthetic gas. The process is illustrated in FIG. 20-3.

The tar residue is collected in a second reaction vessel. This vessel is heated to 1000°F and hydrogen gas is pumped in at 600 lbs per square inch. The hydrogen combines with the tar residue to form a light motor fuel (synthetic gas) and a heavy fuel oil vapor that is led away from the reaction vessel and condensed using fractional distillation.

The residue left from this process is a *char residue*. The char residue can be utilized to make more hydrogen to drive the primary process. This is the simplest method of producing synthetic gas and oil from coal, but it's the least cost effective.

Second method for producing synthetic gas

The process used by the Germans in WWII is called *hydrogenation*. It is a method of reacting coal with hydrogen at high pressure—usually in the presence of a catalyst.

The coal is fed into a reaction vessel in the form of a slurry. A catalyst, such as cobalt molybdenum, is mixed into the slurry. The reaction vessel is heated to a temperature of 850°F and pressurized with hydrogen at 2000 to 4000 psi.

The liquid fraction of the product is distilled to produce a synthetic gas and oil. Unreacted coal is removed from the vessel and gasified to produce hydrogen for the primary reaction.

GOING FURTHER

At least two additional methodologies for manufacturing synthetic gas from coal are possible. Each has its advantages and disadvantages. Also, some processes can convert and enrich the carbon monoxide and hydrogen to methane (natural gas) using a nickel catalyst.

The United States has two trillion tons of recoverable coal. If an economical method of synthetic gas manufacturing could be developed, it would go a long way in helping the United States recover from the high cost of imported crude oil.

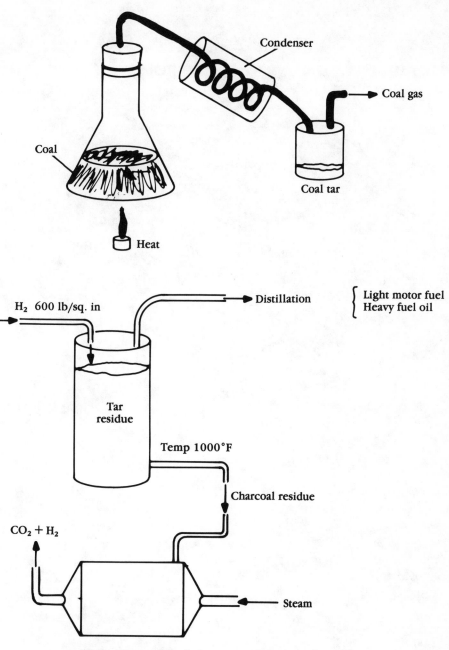

20-3 The schematic for generating synthetic gasoline.

Chapter **21**

Alcohol fuel production

*I*n the early 1970s, our country was subjected to an embargo that was instituted by the league of Arab nations (OPEC). This was a rude awakening for all Americans, who saw our country's energy supply held at ransom until the price of crude oil sky-rocketed.

The high cost of crude oil made alternative energy sources more feasible. One such avenue is alcohol fuel production. Although the price of crude oil is not at the point where it is economically profitable to convert the family car to alcohol, with the information contained here, you always have the option.

The conversion of sugar into alcohol is a simple process, which dates back thousands of years. Yeast are unicellular fungi that can convert dissolved sugar into ethanol and CO_2. The alcohol and carbon dioxide are byproducts of the yeast's digestion of sugar. Yeast secretes an enzyme "zymase" that enables it to digest sugar and promote the chemical reaction. The equation for ethanol production is:

$$C_6H_{12}O_6 \quad Zymase = 2C_2H_5OH + CO_2$$
glucose ethanol carbon dioxide

Yeast is used both in baking as well as in the manufacturing of alcoholic beverages. For baking purposes, the yeast has been bred for carbon dioxide production, which causes baked goods to rise. This type of yeast is called *baker's yeast*. For alcohol production, the yeast has been bred for greater alcohol production, consequently this yeast is called *brewer's yeast*.

For this demonstration, you can use baker's yeast that is available in most supermarkets. Although the alcohol yield will not be as high as if you had used brewer's yeast, the ease and simplicity with which you can purchase baker's yeast makes up for the loss.

SUGAR CONCENTRATION, pH, AND TEMPERATURE

Sugar concentration is important because it is the food source for the yeast. A 16% sugar solution is considered the ideal for yeast. A 9% sugar concentration doesn't provide sufficient food, but a 25% concentration is too much food, which would initiate the yeast to put more energy into reproduction instead of producing alcohol. The ideal pH of the solution should be 4.5 to 5.0. The ideal temperature ranges from 75 to 85 °F.

You can fudge from the ideal yeast environment. It would cost too much in time, labor, and money to provide the ideal environment. You would only meet this criteria if you were pursuing alcohol production on a larger basis.

REACTION VESSEL

Your reaction vessel can be any small jar with a tight-fitting lid. The design is simple (see FIG. 21-1). The tubing and fittings are available from a local tropical fish store. You should use silicone-based tubing (light transparent green), rather than plastic (clear). The reason to use silicone is that the tubing is more flexible.

Fermentation lock

On the vessel is a simple fermentation lock. This "U" shaped tube is partially filled with water. The function of the lock is to allow carbon dioxide to escape, and at the same time prevent oxygen (air) and unwanted organisms from entering the reaction vessel. If air (oxygen) is allowed to enter during fermentation, the yeast will convert the sugar into vinegar (acetic acid), instead of alcohol.

Use a larger diameter tubing than is shown in the illustration or the CO_2 will push the water through the tubing. The fermentation lock is essential to the production of alcohol and also prevents the carbon dioxide from building up to a hazardous pressure.

When running my experiment, I placed a gas-collecting bag on the fermentation lock. I did this for two reasons. The first reason was to measure the carbon dioxide output of the process. The second reason is that it showed that fermentation was occurring, and pinpointed when it stopped (no more gas production). Using a gas-collecting bag is

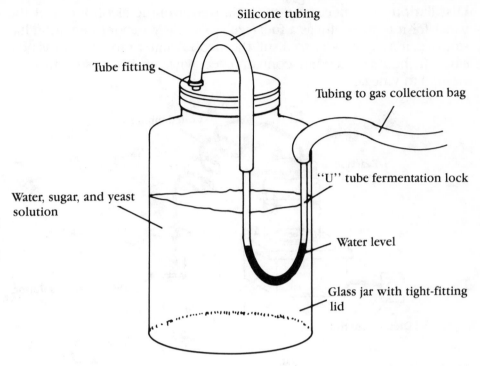

Silicone tubing

Tube fitting

Tubing to gas collection bag

"U" tube fermentation lock

Water, sugar, and yeast solution

Water level

Glass jar with tight-fitting lid

21-1 The reaction vessel.

not essential to carry out the experiment. But if you follow my experiment, note that I used a bag, not a balloon. A balloon would require pressure to inflate, and pressure is not desirable. The bag is folded to remove as much air as possible and requires no pressure to inflate.

Step 1 Mix a tablespoon of sugar per 1/3 pint of water in the reaction vessel. The water temperature should be about 90 °F to get the yeast started. Add a small quantity of baker's yeast to the solution. Close the vessel and attach the tubing to the fermentation lock.

Do not fill the reaction vessel completely. The yeast mixture will foam when it starts production. If the vessel is completely filled, the foam will be forced through the tubing.

Fermentation Fermentation develops quickly. The process is completed in about three days. However, because the yeast has finished working it doesn't mean all the sugar has been converted. The alcohol is toxic to the yeast. Fermentation stops for baker's yeast when the alcohol concentration reaches 8 to 12%. For brewer's yeast, fermentation continues a little longer until the alcohol concentration reaches 10 to 14%.

Distillation   It is necessary to distill (remove) the alcohol out of the water for it to be useful as a fuel (see FIG. 21-2). When fermentation has stopped, it's a good idea to distill the alcohol/water mix as soon as possible. If the mix becomes contaminated with air, it can still turn the alcohol to vinegar.

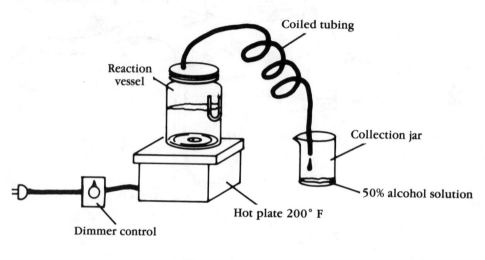

Distillation

21-2   The distillation set-up.

Alcohol is hygroscopic, meaning it readily combines with water. Water boils at 212 °F and ethanol boils at 173 °F. You might think that by raising the temperature of the solution to 175 °F you could boil off (remove) all of the alcohol. Unfortunately, this will not happen. The water and alcohol molecules combine tightly, and heat of vaporization requires additional energy. With all things considered, you should bring the solution to about 200 °F. The majority of the steam will be alcohol and will yield 40 to 50% alcohol. This alcohol concentration is good enough for our purposes and can be used as a fuel for an alcohol lamp.

Remember, if you used a tablespoon of sugar in the reaction vessel, don't expect to distill more than a tablespoon of alcohol. To increase the concentration of alcohol further requires additional distillation steps. By running the finished product from the first distillation through the distillation process at a lower temperature of 190 °F will increase the alcohol concentration to about 65%. Repeating the process again at 180 °F will increase the concentration to about 90% (fuel grade).

Step 2 When fermentation has stopped (in about three days), you must distill the alcohol out of the solution. For this, you need a hot plate and a dimmer control. Hot plates are available in most housewares and hardware stores, the same is true of the dimmer controls. Dimmers are usually used for incandescent lighting; just be sure that the capacity of the dimmer (in watts) equals or exceeds the wattage of the hot plate. Wire the dimmer in the hot plate's line cord. Use an oven thermometer to measure the temperature of the hot plate. Use the dimmer control to calibrate the hot plate's temperature to about 200 °F.

Another method of calibration is to place a cup of water on the hot plate with the thermometer in the water. Use the dimmer control to adjust the water temperature to 200 °F.

With the hot plate calibrated, you can start distilling the solution. Remove the tubing going to the fermentation lock at the top of the reaction vessel. Replace this with a longer coiled section of tubing that leads into a collection jar. The liquid that collects should be about 50% alcohol, which is good enough to use in alcohol lamps.

FUEL GRADE

It is hard to remove water from a 95% alcohol mix. The boiling point of the solution is almost identical to pure ethanol. If you're burning straight alcohol in a gas engine, 5 to 10% water in the alcohol actually improves performance over pure alcohol.

However, if you plan to mix the alcohol with gas to make gasohol, the water content must be reduced to about 1%. Too much water in the gas will cause the gas and alcohol to separate out into layers.

Running fuel-grade (90 to 95%) alcohol in a car is probably easier than you think. Simply enlarge the carburetor jets by 30% and advance the engine timing several degrees and you're ready to go. A little extra equipment is necessary for cool-weather starts (below 50 °F), such as priming the engine with a little gas to start it up. A pre-heater or a heat pick-up off the exhaust manifold will provide warm air for proper alcohol vaporization to keep the engine running smoothly.

The use of ethanol fuels in cars is not new. Henry Ford offered automobiles at the turn of the century that were capable of running on either gas or alcohol.

2-cycle engines

If you want to use alcohol to run smaller 2-cycle gas engines for lawn-mowers and such, it is necessary to mix a vegetable oil in the fuel instead of motor fuel that is used with gas. The reason is that motor oil doesn't mix as well with alcohol as it does with gasoline.

U.S. government regulations

The U.S. government requires that all stills that produce alcohol must be registered. The Bureau of Alcohol, Tobacco, and Firearms has several regional offices across the United States. Call or write for your regional office to:

DEPARTMENT OF THE TREASURY
Bureau of Alcohol, Tobacco and Firearms
Distilled Spirits and Tobacco Branch
650 Massachusetts Ave.
Washington, DC 20226
(202) 927-8210

Contact the regional office for an AFP (alcohol fuel permit) permit. Currently, the AFP permit doesn't cost anything, but another fee is involved. Mention that your still is a demonstration unit that only produces a small amount of fuel alcohol, like 10 ml per run, and they might waive the fee.

GOING FURTHER

This chapter has concentrated on the conversion of sugar to alcohol directly. Starch and cellulose products can also be used to produce alcohol. These products require additional enzyme steps to convert the material to simple sugars for the yeast to convert it to alcohol.

Chapter **22**

Bio-gas generation

*W*aste disposal is a growing problem. Currently, most human waste is released into the planet's water supply with perhaps a little sewage treatment. The pollution has negative effects on all levels of the eco-system. How much better it would be if we could purify this waste and produce a nonpolluting energy source. We can and the added benefit is that the residue from the process is a nutrient-rich fertilizer for plants.

Bio-gas generation plants are currently used in India and Australia. They are most commonly found on rural farms. The rural location adds the incentive to produce one's own power (as much as possible), rather than paying to have it shipped in.

BIO-GAS COMPOSITION

Bio-gas can be generated from human, animal, or vegetable waste. The composition of bio-gas is approximately 50 to 60% methane, 30 to 35% carbon dioxide, 1 to 5% hydrogen, 0.5 to 3% nitrogen, and trace amounts of carbon monoxide, oxygen, and hydrogen sulfide. Bio-gas can be used for heating, cooking and as a fuel supply for gasoline engines (with minor modifications).

Plant fertilizer

The residue from the process is a high-quality nutrient-rich plant fertilizer. This is an important factor. Utilizing the fertilizer, you can create a more closed eco-system that doesn't waste material and is self sufficient. Figure 22-1 shows a closed system.

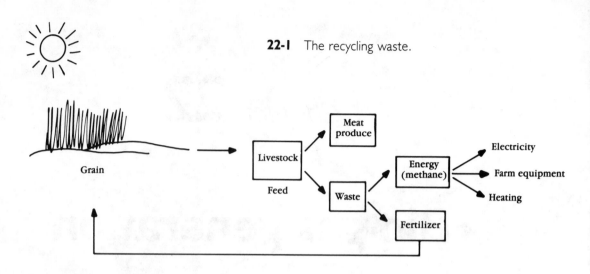

22-1 The recycling waste.

Anaerobic fermentation

Bio-gas is generated by the decomposition of organic material (manure or human feces and/or vegetable waste) in the absence of oxygen (air). In this respect, it is similar to alcohol production. If you allow oxygen into the alcohol fermentation process, vinegar instead of alcohol will be produced. With bio-gas generation, oxygen in the process will produce ammonia instead of methane gas.

Vegetable waste produces (on average) 7 times more methane gas than animal waste. Digesters have been designed that work primarily on plant material, but additional nitrogen must be added to the mix.

Temperature and acidity The ideal temperature for the anaerobic digestion of waste is 85 to 105 °F. Although digestion can still occur from a temperature range of 50 to 120 °F, it will proceed much slower. The ideal acidity is 6.8 to 8.0 pH.

Carbon to nitrogen ratio To maximize the process, the ratio should be 30 parts carbon to 1 part nitrogen. The bacteria consume carbon 30 times faster than nitrogen. Having the proper ratio ensures complete digestion of the raw materials, provided that it has maximum gas production and a residue (plant fertilizer) with the highest nutrient value. Animal waste usually has a high nitrogen content, and vegetable waste usually has a higher carbon content.

TEST EXPERIMENT

For this small test experiment, do not be concerned with trying to set the ideal environment for anaerobic digestion. Any small bottle with a

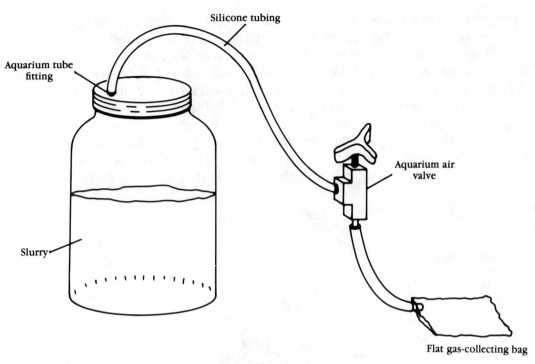

22-2 The reaction vessel.

tight-fitting lid can be used for a digester (see FIG. 22-2). Mix some manure and water to form a slurry. Add the slurry mixture to the digester. Do not fill the digester to the top because it might foam as the bacteria gets to work. If you wish, add a small amount of sawdust to the slurry to increase the carbon content. The sawdust is optional; the digester will produce bio-gas without it. However, if you do add sawdust, make sure that it is from "real" wood and not from particleboard or wood composite. Wood composites contain resins and epoxies that might halt gas production. The output of the digester is fed through an aquarium air valve into a gas-collecting bag.

The digester should be held at a temperature of 80 to 90°F. You could use an aquarium heater and a water jacket to keep the digester at this optimum temperature. Otherwise, you can place the digester in a warm section of your home or apartment, perhaps near a heating vent, furnace, or hot-water tank.

Gas production usually begins within 21 days. Whenever you test for methane gas, wear safety goggles. When the unit first begins producing gas, it will be mostly carbon dioxide. To test for methane production, close the air valve and remove the bag section, keep the tubing to the bag crimped or folded at this point to prevent any gas from escaping from the bag. Hold a lit match near the free end of the tubing and release the crimp. Carbon dioxide will not burn. Continue to test the gas production every day or so until the match ignites the escaping gas. Remember to open the air valve after you reconnect the gas-collecting bag or you might find an undesirable clean-up job waiting for you the next time you check on the digester.

When you are producing methane, allow the gas to collect in the bag. You can construct a simple burner (see FIG. 22-3) to burn your collected gas. When you are burning the methane gas, you can make a

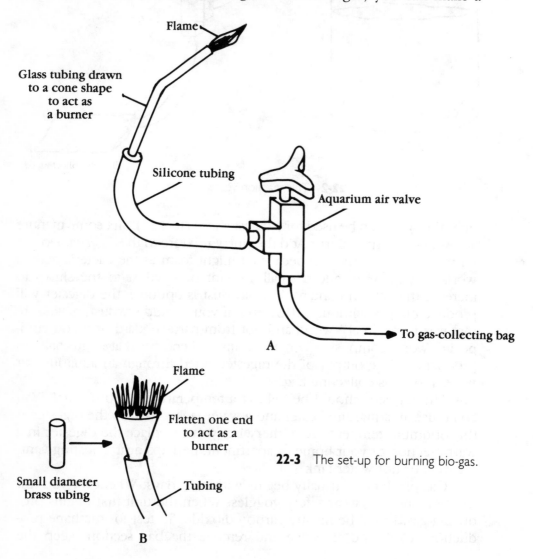

22-3 The set-up for burning bio-gas.

more spectacular demonstration by squeezing the bag to increase gas pressure.

When your digester has stopped producing gas, the residue left in the bottle is an excellent fertilizer for your plants.

GOING FURTHER

The most obvious avenue for research is sewage treatment plants. Biogas plants cannot only produce their own nonpolluting power, but are ecologically sound investments.

Chapter 23

Wood as fuel

You might think wood is already a fuel. Wood-burning stoves and ovens are common, but did you know that you could run gasoline engines on wood? The method to extract a motor fuel from wood is simple. You can distill wood alcohol (methanol alcohol) or a gaseous hydrocarbon from wood. Running gasoline-powered vehicles from wood isn't a new idea, during World War II, civilians in Europe did so. Modifications to the carburetor were necessary for the engine to run this type of gaseous fuel.

EXPERIMENTAL GAS GENERATOR

Figure 23-1 illustrates the simple gas generator. The generator is filled with sawdust or small wood chips. It's important to use real or natural wood material. Particle board and other wood substitutes contain resins and epoxies that might develop harmful fumes.

Heat the sawdust in the enclosed test tube. The gas generated is fed into a gas-collecting bag. When the wood is completely utilized, close the air valve and disconnect the generator. Replace the generator with a gas burner (see FIG. 23-2). Wearing safety goggles, open the valve and use an ignited match to light the escaping gases.

The gas composition is a mixture of carbon monoxide and hydrogen, with a small amount of methane and carbon dioxide. The residue left is mostly carbon and can be utilized by another process, such as by a carbon source for the bio-gas generator.

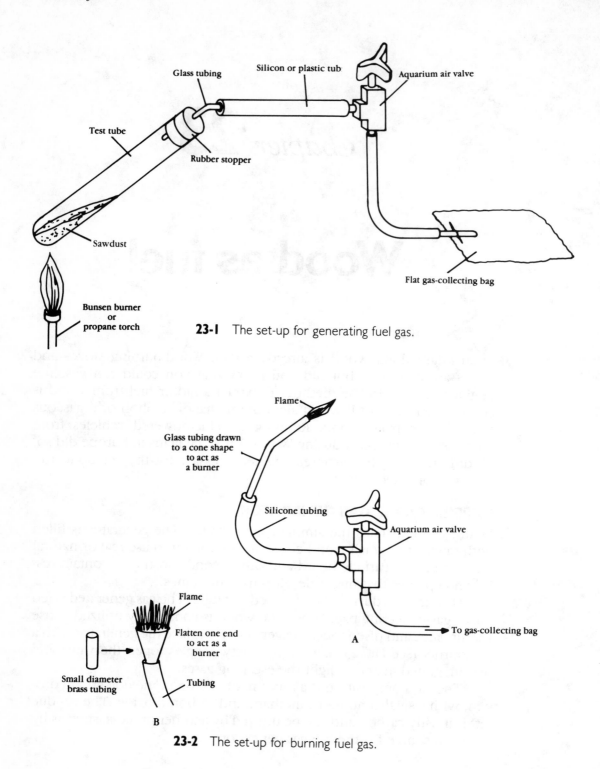

Glass tubing

Silicon or plastic tub

Aquarium air valve

Test tube

Rubber stopper

Sawdust

Flat gas-collecting bag

Bunsen burner
or
propane torch

23-1   The set-up for generating fuel gas.

Flame

Glass tubing drawn
to a cone shape
to act as
a burner

Silicone tubing

Aquarium air valve

Flame

Flatten one end
to act as a
burner

Small diameter
brass tubing

Tubing

A

To gas-collecting bag

B

23-2   The set-up for burning fuel gas.

Index

A

air-pollution monitor, 105-112
  additional uses, 110-111
  circuit, 108-110
  gas sensor, 105-106
  parts list, 111
  sensors, 105-108
alcohol fuel
  2-cycle engines, 205
  distillation, 204
  fermentation, 203
  fermentation lock, 202-203
  grade, 205
  producing, 201-206
  reaction vessel, 202-205
  sugar concentration/pH/temperature, 202
  U.S. government regulations, 206
Allegro Electronic Systems, 73, 111, 158
alpha particles, 64
amino acids, 2
astrophotography, equatorial camera mount, 133-145
atomic particles, viewing, 89-92
autonomic physiology, 39
axons, 114

B

Babarbo, Danielo, 183
Babcock, W., 83
Baker, K. L., 83
baker's yeast, 201
Becker, Robert, 47-48
Becquerel, Henri, 64
Berg, Paul, 12-13
beta particles, 64
Beuhler, William, 93
bio-feedback device, 39-44
  circuit construction, 42-43
  circuit description, 39
  circuit operation, 43-44
  electrodes, 41-42
  parts list, 44
bio-gas, 207-211
  anaerobic fermintation, 208
  carbon to nitrogen ratio, 208
  composition, 207-208
  plant fertilizer, 207-208
  temperature and acidity, 208
  test experiment, 208-211
biological neurons, 114-118
brain, human, 115 (see also neural networks)
brewer's yeast, 201

C

Carolina Biological Supply Company, 26, 92
Cattaneo, A. G., 83
Chang, Annie, 13
Chikarmane, Herman, 31
clones, 9
coal
  buying, 196-197
  caution statement, 197-198
  char residue, 198
  hydrogeneration, 198
  making synthetic gasoline/oil, 195-199
  nondestructive distillation, 196
codons, 7
  anti-, 7
Cohen, Stanley, 13
Crick, Francis, 4

D

Da Vinci, Leonardo, 183
dendrites, 114
Deoxyribonucleic Acid (*see* DNA)
Department of the Treasury, 206
DNA, 1-26
  clones, 9
  double helix structure, 4
  gene splicing experiment, 15-26
  genetic engineering, 11
  genetic manipulation by viruses, 10-11
  human genome project, 2-15
  ligation, 20-21
  protein synthesis, 6-7
  recombinant, 12-13
  repairing damaged, 31
  restriction endonuclease enzymes, 13-14
  sticky ends, 12
  transforming E. coli with recombinant, 21-23

E

E. coli, 9, 12, 14
  growing, 17-20
Edmund Scientific, 57

ELF
  computer monitors, 48-49, 51
  effects on cells, 46-47
  electric blankets, 50
  electric clocks, 51-52
  electric heaters, 52
  electric shavers, 50
  fluorescent lights, 51
  hair dryers, 52
  precautions around the home, 50-52
  radiation, 45-55
  research evidence, 47-48
  shielding, 49-50
  television, 51
ELF monitor, 52-55
  calibration, 54
  circuit, 52-54
  construction, 54
  parts list, 55
  using, 54-55
enzymes, 3
  HindII, 11
  restriction endonuclease, 13-14
equatorial camera mount, 133-145
  additional uses, 144
  battery, 141
  camera arm, 137
  circuit, 137-139
  constructing, 135-137
  film speed and aperture, 144
  flexible shaft, 140-141
  light pollution, 144
  parts list, 145
  using, 142-144
expansion cloud chamber, 89-92
  constructing, 89
  radioactive source, 90
  using, 90-91
experiments (*see also* projects)
  bio-gas, 207-211
  expansion cloud chamber, 89-92
  extracting gas from wood, 213-214
  gas generator, 213-214
  gene splicing, 15-26
  genetic evolution, 27-31
  plasma acoustics, 83-87
extremely low-frequency magnetic field (*see* ELF)

F

Franklin, Rosalind, 4
fuel
   alcohol, 201-206
   synthetic gas/oil, 195-199
   wood, 213-214

G

gamma rays, 64-65
gas generator, experimental, 213-214
gases, 105-106
   bio-, 207-211
gasoline, synthetic, 195-199
Geiger counter, 64, 67-73
   checking/troubleshooting, 70-71
   circuit, 67-68
   constructing, 68-70
   detecting solar flares, 72
   inverse square law, 71
   parts list, 72
   radioactive sources, 70
   tubes, 65-66, 71
Geiger-Muller (GM) tube, 65-66
gene splicing experiment, 15-26
   culture plate, 18-20
   disinfecting work area, 18
   E. coli incubator, 17-18
   heat shocking bacteria, 18
   kit, 16-17, 26
   ligation of DNA, 20-21
   overview, 15-17
   results of culture plates, 23-26
   transforming E. coli with recombinant DNA, 21-23
genes
   DNA, 1-26
   manipulating, 1-26
   RNA, 3, 6-9
genetic code, 7
genetic engineering, 11
genetic evolution experiment, 27-31
   culture plates, 28-30
   evolution and sex, 30-31
   kit, 27, 31
   procedure, 27-28
Goldhaber, Marilyn, 51

H

Hiat, Robert, 51
Higg, 14
holograms
   choosing an object, 164-165
   developing, 166-167
   dual channel, 171-172
   making the exposure, 166
   multiplex, 171-172
   producing, 151
   real/virtual images, 168-170
   shooting, 164-172
   viewing, 167-168
holography, 147-173
   additional information, 172
   chemical disposal, 171
   film, 162-163
   general information, 147
   isolation table, 159-161
   laser power supply, 152-158
   optical components and mounts, 161-162
   parts list, 172-173
   producing a hologram, 151
   safelight, 163-164
   shooting a hologram, 164-172
   tips, 170-171
   troubleshooting, 170
   vs. photography, 148-152
   audio amplifier, 58-59
   parts list, 61
   specification, 57-58
   using, 59-60

I

images
   orthoscopic, 169
   pseudoscopic, 170
   real and virtual, 168-170
Images Company, 38, 44, 57, 73, 81, 87, 132, 145, 158, 173, 182
inverse square law, 71
ion generator, negative, 36-38
ions
   negative, 33-38
   positive effects, 33-36
   thermal ionization, 75-76, 84
isolation table, 159-161

J

John Hopkins University, 48

K

Kirlian, Semyon, 175
Kirlian, Valentina, 175
Kirlian photography, 175-182
    circuit construction, 177-180
    circuit operation, 176-177
    exposure plate, 178-180
    exposures, 180-182
    film, 181-182
    history, 175-176
    parts list, 182
    usefulness, 176

L

laser, 151
    safety, 157
laser light, 151-152
laser power supply, 152-158
    connecting to laser, 153-154
    how it works, 153
    parts list, 157
    testing/calibrating, 154-155
    tube housing, 155-157
Leeper, Ed, 47
lie detector, 39-44
    circuit construction, 42-43
    circuit description, 39
    circuit operation, 43-44
    electrodes, 41-42
    parts list, 44
light-pollution filter, 144-145

M

magnetohydrodynamic (*see* MHD)
Mandel, 14
Maryland Department of Health and
    Hygiene, 48
Matther, 7
messenger RNA (mRNA), 6-7
MHD generator, 75-81
    advantages, 76
    basics, 75-76
    improving, 79
    liquid metal, 79
    making a plasma, 75-76
    model, 76-78
    operating, 78
    parts list, 81
    propulsion systems, 80-81
Michod, Richard, 31
Mondo-Tronics, 103
Mouser Electronics, 158

N

Nathans, Daniel, 11
negative ion generator, 36-38
    parts list, 38
neural networks, 113-122
    additional uses, 120-121
    biological neurons, 114-117
    computer modeling, 117
    electronic neurons, 117-118
    factors to program, 113-114
    parts list, 122
    sun-tracker circuit, 118-120
neurons, 114-118
    biological, 114-117
    electronic, 117-118
Nirenberg, 7
nitinol-SMA, 93-103
    activating wire, 96-97
    additional applications, 100-101
    annealing phase, 95
    applications, 94
    circuit, 97
    demonstration, 97-99
    direct electric heating, 96-97
    how it works, 94-95
    martensitic phase, 94-95
    parent phase, 94
    parts list, 102
    properties, 95-96
    pulse-width modulation heating, 97
    using, 99-100
    wire diameter, 96
nucleic acids, 3-4 (*see also* DNA; RNA)
Nucleus Company (The), 73, 92

O

oil, synthetic, 195-199
Olander, Arne, 93
Ostrander, Sheila, 175

P

peptides, 2
photography
　astro-, 133-145
　holography (*see* holograms; hologra-
　　phy)
　Kirlian, 175-182
　pinhole, 183-194
pinhole photography, 183-194
　camera, 184-188
　darkroom, 188-193
　developing film, 190-192
　exposure, 189-190
　exposure times, 194
　F-stop, 187
　finishing the camera, 188
　history, 183
　loading the camera, 189
　making the pinhole, 187-188
　paper negative, 192-193
plasma acoustics, 83-87
　basic operation, 83-84
　experimenting with, 84-86
　improving the design, 87
　parts list, 87
plasmids, 12, 15
　constructing, 15-17
　pAMP, 15
Polen, Michael, 51
polypeptide molecule, 2
polypeptides, 2
projects (*see also* experiments)
　air-pollution monitor, 105-112
　bio-feedback device, 39-44
　ELF monitor, 52-55
　equatorial camera mount, 133-145
　Geiger counter, 67-73
　holograms, 159-173
　hydrophone, 57-61
　isolation table for holography, 159-
　　161
　Kirlian photography, 176-182
　laser power supply for holography,
　　147-158
　lie detector, 39-44
　making synthetic gasoline/oil from
　　coal, 195-199
　MHD generator, 75-81

negative ion generator, 36-38
neural networks, 113-122
pinhole photography, 184-194
producing alcohol fuel, 201-206
stepper motors, 123-132
pulse-width modulation (PWM), 97

R

radiation
　ELF, 45-55
　Geiger counter, 67-73
radioactivity, 63-64
　background radiation, 63-64
　history, 64-65
　inverse square law, 71
　measuring, 65
　sources, 70
Ribonucleic Acid (*see* RNA)
ribosomal RNA, 7-9
RNA, 3, 6
　messenger (mRNA), 6-7
　protein synthesis, 8
　ribosomal, 7-9
　transfer (tRNA), 7
rotor, 124

S

Savitz, David, 48
Schroeder, Lynn, 175
sensors
　characteristics, 107-108
　future, 106-107
　gas, 105-106
shaped memory alloy (SMA), 93
　history, 93-94
　nitinol, 93-103
shaped memory effect (SME), 93
Smith, 11
solar flares, detecting, 72
Soyka, Fred, 33
stator, 124
stepper motors, 123-132
　basic operation, 123-125
　checking/troubleshooting, 131-132
　circuit, 129-132
　half stepping, 125
　parts list, 132

stepper motors *cont.*
   real world, 125-128
   resolution, 124-125
   types of, 125
synapse, 114

T

temperature, transition, 94
thermal ionization, 75, 84
transcription process, 6
transfer RNA (tRNA), 7
transition temperature, 94
Tribukait, Dr. Bernard, 47

V

viruses
   genetic manipulation, 10-11
   simian virus 40 (SV40), 11

W

Watson, James, 4
Wertheimer, Dr. Nancy, 47, 50
white-light reflection, 149
Wilcox, 11
wood, extracting gas from, 213-214

Y

yeast, 201

Other Bestsellers of Related Interest

EXPERIMENTS IN GALLIUM ARSENIDE TECHNOLOGY
D.J. Branning and Dave Prochnow

One of the fastest growing areas in electronics technology! Twenty-five challenging projects demonstrate the technology of gallium arsenide (GaAs) in this fascinating resource book. Now you can explore, firsthand, the products, manufacturers, and technologies that contribute to the GaAs microelectronics and optoelectronics industries. 256 pages, 207 illustrations. **Book No. 3052, $16.95 paperback, $24.95 hardcover**

ELECTRONIC COMPONENTS:
A Complete Reference for Project Builders
Delton T. Horn

Armed with this book and a manufacturer's spec sheet, you can get the most out of almost any electronic component. This benchtop reference contains practical information on all kinds of electronic components used by today's hobbyists. It catalogs characteristics, specifications, and component uses that range in complexity from basic wire and solder to transistors and ICs. And it presents insights into the theory and operation of components in typical circuit designs, the pros and cons of using devices in various situations, where and how to find parts, and criteria for making substitutions. 328 pages, 300 illustrations. **Book No. 3671, $18.95 paperback, $29.95 hardcover**

THE LASER COOKBOOK: 88 Practical Projects
Gordon McComb

The laser is one of the most important inventions to come along this half of the 20th Century. This book provides 88 laser-based projects that are geared toward the garage-shop tinkerer on a limited budget. The projects vary from experimenting with laser optics and constructing a laser optical bench to using lasers for light shows, gunnery practice, even beginning and advanced holography. 400 pages, 356 illustrations. **Book No. 3090, $19.95 paperback only**

49 EASY ELECTRONIC PROJECTS FOR TRANSCONDUCTANCE & NORTON OP AMPS
Delton T. Horn

The projects cover a wide range of practical applications from DC amplifiers to current switches, voltage regulators to Schmitt triggers, and more. Each includes easy-to-follow instructions, and most can be constructed in a single evening costing less than $15 to build. Delton T. Horn gives you all the information you need to use transconductance and Norton op amps in your projects. 230 pages, 163 illustrations. **Book No. 3455, $16.95 paperback, $25.95 hardcover**

TIPS & TECHNIQUES FOR ELECTRONICS EXPERIMENTERS—2nd Edition
Don Tuite and Delton T. Horn

Packed with practical circuit-building tips and techniques, this completely revised and updated edition of a classic experimenter's guide also provides you with ten complete projects. These include a random number generator, an electronic organ, and a deluxe logic probe. Covering such basics as soldering and mounting components, finding and correcting malfunctions and making practical component substitutions, this book also covers the use of breadboards and techniques for finishing your projects. 160 pages, 83 illustrations. **Book No. 3145, $12.95 paperback only**

101 OPTOELECTRONIC PROJECTS
Delton T. Horn

Discover the broad range of practical applications for optoelectronic devices! Here's a storehouse of practical optoelectronic projects just waiting to be put to use. Horn features 101 new projects including: power circuits, control circuits, sound circuits, flasher circuits, display circuits, game circuits, and many other fascinating projects. This book offers you an opportunity to make a hands-on investigation of the practical potential of optoelectronic devices. 240 pages, 273 illustrations. **Book No. 3205, $24.95 hardcover only**

600 LOW-COST ELECTRONIC CIRCUITS
David M. Gauthier

Need just the right circuit—FAST? Then look no further! This "nuts and bolts" resource tool is packed with illustrations, schematics, and hundreds of the most current application circuits. The author has compiled over 600 practical circuits that you can build or adapt to your own electronic projects. And, most of these useful circuits can be built for $25 or less! All of the circuits use between one and 10 hobby-type ICs, and their applications range from digital gates to FM receivers. 350 pages, 698 illustrations. **Book No. 3219, $18.95 paperback only**

VIDEO, STEREO AND OPTOELECTRONICS:
18 Advanced Electronic Projects
Rudolf F. Graf and William Sheets

With the challenging projects included here, you can produce devices that are both modern in design and genuinely useful. You'll find projects for wireless headphones, FM stereo and TV transmitters, receivers for longwave and FM broadcast bands, and more. Each project includes step-by-step construction plans, parts lists, and working diagrams. None of these plans calls for expensive or hard-to-get components. 368 pages, 216 illustrations. **Book No. 3358, $18.95 paperback, $28.95 hardcover**

ANALOG SWITCHES: Applications and Projects
Delton T. Horn

For more complex functions that demand speed and accuracy, an analog switch is essential. Delton Horn explains what analog switching circuits are and how to use them. Fifteen practical projects give you hands-on experience with the switching circuits presented. Easy to understand, this book is a valuable resource that contains all the information you need to build and modify your own analog switches. 160 pages, 114 illustrations. **Book No. 3445, $12.95 paperback, $21.95 hardcover**

HOMEMADE LIGHTNING:
Creative Experiments in Electricity
R. A. Ford

Packed with fascinating facts, this book combines scientific history, electronics theory, and practical experiments to introduce you to the evolving science of electrostatics. The abundant illustrations and varied collection of creative, hands-on projects reveal the wide-ranging impact of electrostatics on motor design, plant growth, medicine, aerodynamics, photography, meteorology, and gravity research. 208 pages, 111 illustrations. **Book No. 3576, $14.95 paperback only**

THE ELECTRONICS WORKBENCH:
Tools, Testers, and Tips for the Hobbyist
Delton T. Horn

Not only does Horn offer important information about arranging the workbench, construction tips, and electronic safety, he also gives you guidelines for using a wide variety of equipment. He takes an in-depth look at each major category of test instrument, explaining the characteristics and power capabilities of various models and giving you a reliable set of guidelines with which to choose the right equipment. 264 pages, 125 illustrations. **Book No. 3672, $18.95 paperback only**

HOME REMOTE-CONTROL AND AUTOMATION PROJECTS—2nd Edition
Delton T. Horn

Fifteen all-new projects expand the outstanding collection that made the first edition a worldwide favorite among electronics hobbyists. You'll find a complete selection of door and window controllers, temperature controllers, liquid monitors and controllers, stereo and TV projects, telephone-related projects, controller motors, electronic switching units, timers, wireless controllers, and a computer controller—complete with programming information. 320 pages, 240 illustrations. **Book No. 3765, $18.95 paperback, $29.95 hardcover**

DESIGNING AND BUILDING ELECTRONIC FILTERS—Deluxe Edition

Delton T. Horn

This book covers almost every imaginable type of filter circuit, ranging from simple passive filter networks to sophisticated digital filters. You'll explore the four basic types of filter circuits—low-pass, high-pass, band-pass, and band-reject—and specialized filter types. Whether you're novice or an old hand with a soldering iron, this book covers building electronic filters for every purpose. 320 pages, 178 illustrations. **Book No. 3887, $26.95 hardcover only**

TROUBLESHOOTING AND REPAIRING ELECTRONIC MUSIC SYNTHESIZERS

Delton T. Horn

Delton T. Horn, noted electronics expert and author of more than 35 electronics titles, gives you complete, step-by-step instructions for servicing or replacing all synthesizer components and circuitry—including those found in both older analog devices and today's most advanced digital systems. you'll get concise background information, circuit specifications, and instructions that will help you to troubleshoot even the most difficult problems in a hurry, and make quick and easy repairs. 224 pages, 97 illustrations. **Book No. 3888, $16.95 paperback, $26.95 hardcover**

Prices Subject to Change Without Notice.

Look for These and Other TAB Books at Your Local Bookstore

To Order Call Toll Free 1-800-822-8158
(24-hour telephone service available.)

or write to TAB Books, Blue Ridge Summit, PA 17294-0840.

Title	Product No.	Quantity	Price

☐ Check or money order made payable to TAB Books

Charge my ☐ VISA ☐ MasterCard ☐ American Express

Acct. No. _____ Exp. _____

Signature: _____

Name: _____

Address: _____

City: _____

State: _____ Zip: _____

Subtotal $ _____

Postage and Handling
($3.00 in U.S., $5.00 outside U.S.) $ _____

Add applicable state and local
sales tax $ _____

TOTAL $ _____

TAB Books catalog free with purchase; otherwise send $1.00 in check or money order and receive $1.00 credit on your next purchase.

Orders outside U.S. must pay with international money order in U.S. dollars drawn on a U.S. bank.

TAB Guarantee: If for any reason you are not satisfied with the book(s) you order, simply return it (them) within 15 days and receive a full refund. BC